Memorable Milestone Birthdays

48 Theme Parties to Help You Celebrate

Robin Kring

Meadowbrook Press

Distributed by Simon & Schuster
New York

Library of Congress Cataloging-in-Publication Data
Kring, Robin.
Memorable milestone birthdays: 48 theme parties to help you celebrate/Robin Kring.
p. cm.
ISBN 0-88166-364-6 (Meadowbrook) ISBN 0-743-21242-8 (Simon & Schuster)
1. Birthdays. 2. Entertaining. I. Title

GT2430 .K75 2001
793.2—dc21 00-045202
CIP

Managing Editor: Christine Zuchora-Walske
Editor: Megan McGinnis
Proofreader: Laurie Eckblad Anderson
Production Manager: Paul Woods
Desktop Publishing: Danielle White
Cover Art: Doug Oudekerk
Illustrations: John Clarke
Index: Beverlee Day

Published by Meadowbrook Press, 5451 Smetana Drive, Minnetonka, Minnesota 55343

www.meadowbrookpress.com

BOOK TRADE DISTRIBUTION by Simon & Schuster, a division of Simon and Schuster, Inc., 1230 Avenue of the Americas, New York, New York 10020

05 04 03 02 01 10 9 8 7 6 5 4 3 2 1

Printed in the United States of America

DEDICATION

For Robert Paul

ACKNOWLEDGMENTS

Thank you to Mom and Dad, who inspired their
"April Fool" baby with many happy birthday memories.

Preface

I was born on April Fools' Day, so my birthday celebrations have always been blessed with practical jokes. Some past birthday gifts I received were a cardboard box covered with chocolate frosting, a plastic banana containing a pair of earrings, and eighteen nesting boxes with the smallest one containing a gift check. I received that last gift for my eighteenth birthday, and my friends and family loved watching me rip open each box, laughing as I discovered another one to unwrap. Of course, after I unwrapped each box, they all shouted, "April Fool!"

As you see, my birth date lends my birthday celebrations an obvious theme. And my family loved to celebrate them that way—especially milestone birthdays. On my thirteenth birthday, a family friend gave me thirteen small wrapped boxes, each containing a gift. One box contained a gift from my mom: a diamond ring. The gift was a family heirloom passed down each generation to the eldest (or, in my case, only) girl on her thirteenth birthday. My mother received it on her thirteenth birthday from her mother, who had received it from her mother on her thirteenth birthday. And now the ring was mine.

My mother was also the one who introduced me to the art of party making. I took to it with passion. I recall requesting a birthday cake decorated with the faces of the Monkees for my first theme birthday party. Several fun, unique theme birthday parties followed. And planning unusual theme birthday parties is now part of my personal and professional life. In this book I'll share some of my favorite milestone birthday party themes with you.

I wish you many happy milestone moments!

Robin Kring

Contents

Introduction

Although every birthday is special, some birthdays mark turning points in life. Different cultures designate different birthdays as milestones. The Jewish culture considers the twelfth or thirteenth birthday the one on which boys and girls become adults, and a child prepares for months to become a bar or bat mitzvah (a son or daughter of the commandments) to mark the milestone. The Dutch denote even-numbered birthdays as "crown years" during which the honoree receives extraspecial gifts and has his or her dining chair decorated with flowers. The Japanese celebrate certain birthdays with a visit to a local shrine.

The American culture has its milestone birthdays, too. The twenty-first birthday marks the point at which a young person may legally partake of all the perks of adulthood. The thirtieth, fortieth, and fiftieth birthdays all vie for the dubious honor of making the honoree over-the-hill. And the first and one hundredth birthdays are "bookend" milestones.

Each milestone birthday calls for a unique celebration: a milestone birthday party! *Memorable Milestone Birthdays* offers forty-eight creative themes for parties to help you make a dozen milestone birthdays unforgettable. Inside you'll find:

- Step-by-step party planning tips, including a time- and sanity-saving checklist
- Outlines for four theme parties for each milestone birthday, including creative theme-inspired ideas for invitations, décor, activities, menus, birthday cakes and desserts, party favors and prizes, and gifts for the honoree
- Suggestions for planning surprise parties and parties for the very young and old
- An extensive supplier resource directory to help you locate unusual items or services

Although I've chosen twelve milestone birthdays, keep in mind that these theme party ideas can work for *any* birthday. If your basketball-loving son wants a special party to celebrate becoming a bar mitzvah, the Slam Dunk Celebration could be the perfect party theme. Or maybe your best friend has just made some big changes in her life, and a Sizzling Soirée is just the right way to commemorate her forty-second birthday.

And don't feel as if you must use every idea given for a party. Mixing and matching ideas will help you tailor a celebration so it fits the honoree to a tee and will be one guests will talk about for years to come.

PIECE-OF-CAKE PARTY PLANNING TIPS

With this step-by-step guide, planning a magnificent milestone birthday party is as easy as baking a cake.

Step 1: Choose a Flavor for Your Party

From the following chapters, select a party theme that suits the honoree. If the party isn't a surprise, ask the honoree about available dates. To get the best attendance, also consider polling guests for acceptable party dates. If you want to hold the party somewhere other than your home, choose a venue that best fits your party needs and secure it early (at least two months before the party date). If you'll be requiring a caterer, entertainer, florist, photographer, and so on, make reservations with them early, too. Get agreements in writing. When placing orders and working with service vendors, follow up and then follow up again.

Step 2: Invite the Partygoers

The invitation sets the tone for the entire party, and eye-catching invitations help increase attendance. Wouldn't you want to find out what's in store at a party advertised by an invitation attached to a black silk stocking?

Be sure to include the following items on invitations: party date, time, and address (including directions); your name, address, and phone number; any theme information; and a date by which guests should RSVP. To get a good response, send invitations at least three weeks before the party date.

Package invitations properly. If you're making your invitations, design them to fit into a particular envelope. It's maddening to realize after you've made fantastic invitations that you can't find an envelope that fits them. For a really extraordinary statement, consider sending unique invitations without additional packing. The United States Postal Service allows any legal and safe item, such as a high-top sneaker, to be sent through the mail as long as it's properly addressed. Delivery services and hand-delivery are other options. Double-check required postage before mailing.

Step 3: Measure and Mix Party Ingredients

Adapt the décor, activity, and menu to fit your party. Sometimes less is more, so don't feel as if you must use every suggestion listed for a particular party. Also keep in mind that you needn't schedule activities for every moment between eating and opening gifts. Choose activities that fit within the party time and suit your guests' personalities. Remember that sometimes the best party activities—eating scrumptious refreshments, listening to great background music, and mingling among good friends and interesting strangers—occur naturally. Select refreshments that fit your guest list and venue. If you won't have enough tables and chairs to accommodate all your guests, don't serve refreshments that require a knife. And of course, be sure to add your own creative décor, activity, and refreshment ideas to the party plans I've provided.

Step 4: Make the Party

Attend to as many details as possible early on. Recruit volunteers to help you. (Working with others makes planning faster and more fun.) Buy or make decorations and supplies as soon as you decide on a theme. Check RSVPs to determine the number of guests. Check that you have on hand enough tables, chairs, tableware, and so on. Prepare as much of the menu as possible beforehand. Wrap your gift, prizes, and favors. Clean the house. Place orders and follow up on them frequently. Decorate the party room the day before the party.

Step 5: Add the Frosting

On the day of the party, prepare the rest of the menu and add final decorating touches. To keep your sanity, have a volunteer run last-minute errands. You'll need to stay focused on the party site. Dress for the party at least 1½ hours before guests arrive and have some hors d'oeuvres and beverages ready for early arrivals. Relax with volunteers about an hour before guests arrive. (You'll enjoy the party more after you've had a moment to unwind.) Then greet your guests and get ready to throw a memorable milestone birthday party!

Tip

As you plan and organize your party, walk through these steps periodically to make sure you've covered every detail. The checklist on the next page will help you keep track of your party-in-the-making. And once you've done your best to plan ahead, expect—and accept—the unexpected. Don't let a minor, or for that matter, a major detail spoil the party. Even if something disastrous happens, like the dog eating your roast, make the best of it. Order pizza and consider it something you'll look back on and laugh about. The incident may become a cherished milestone birthday memory.

Checklist

Two to Three Months before the Party

❑ Decide on a theme.
❑ Select a party date and time.
❑ Prepare a guest list.
❑ Choose a location and secure a venue.
❑ If necessary, hire a caterer, entertainer, and florist, and order rentals.
❑ Hire a photographer and/or videographer or recruit volunteers to provide these services.

One Month before the Party

❑ Buy or make invitations.

Three Weeks before the Party

❑ Double-check the required postage for invitations.
❑ Have someone proofread the invitations for missing details and typographical errors.
❑ Mail the invitations.
❑ Recruit volunteers to help you with party duties, such as buying supplies, picking up special orders, preparing the menu, and so on.
❑ Plan the menu.
❑ Plan the activities and prizes.
❑ Decide on your gift. (Allow more time if you plan to make your gift.)

Two Weeks before the Party

❑ Make or buy decorations.
❑ Order the centerpiece and other fresh flowers, if necessary.
❑ Buy or complete your gift. (Wrap it now and avoid the last-minute rush!)
❑ Prepare your shopping list for menu ingredients.
❑ Place deli orders and/or order cake.

One Week before the Party

❑ Follow up with service vendors and special orders.
❑ Clean the house.
❑ Make sure all appropriate serving dishes and utensils are on hand.
❑ Make sure enough tableware is on hand.
❑ Make sure enough tables and chairs are on hand.
❑ Wash and dry table linens if necessary.
❑ Check RSVPs to determine the number of guests.
❑ Buy all groceries except perishables.
❑ Prepare as much of your menu as possible.
❑ Prepare the name tags and place cards. (Make extras for last-minute changes.)
❑ Buy film, tapes, and batteries for cameras and video cameras.

The Day before the Party

❑ Make or pick up cake or dessert.
❑ Pick up special orders.
❑ Buy perishables.
❑ Set tables and decorate the party room.
❑ Assemble items that will be used for activities.
❑ Wrap the prizes.
❑ Make sure your gift is wrapped.
❑ Lay out party clothes.
❑ Mentally walk through the party to make sure everything's covered.

The Day of the Party

❑ Finish last-minute cleaning.
❑ Buy ice or have it delivered.
❑ Prepare the rest of your menu.

Last-Minute Details

❑ Get dressed at least 1½ hours before guests are expected to arrive.
❑ Set out some hors d'oeuvres for early arrivals and have beverages ready to serve.
❑ Relax and chat with volunteers an hour or so before guests arrive.
❑ Greet guests and have a great time!

SURPRISE PARTY SUCCESS

Throwing a surprise party is a favorite way to celebrate someone's milestone birthday. Although planning a surprise party takes work, seeing that amazed look on the honoree's face is worth every ounce of extra effort. Of course, to make the party a surprise, all planning must be done without the honoree's knowledge. So it's helpful to recruit volunteers to help you with planning, decorating, and so on.

Here are more suggestions to make your surprise party a success:

- If you live with the honoree, keep party details a secret by addressing invitations, making decorations and favors, preparing party food, and so on at a friend's house. Or let the honoree help plan the party, but let him or her think the party is for someone else.
- Hold the party a few days before or after the honoree's birthday. Or throw the party at an nontraditional party hour, such as early in the morning.
- If you hold the party in the honoree's home, you'll have to come up with a convincing reason to get him or her out of the house long enough for volunteers to decorate, set out refreshments, and so on. You'll also need a convincing reason for the honoree to return at a certain time. If you hold the party at another site, simply tell the honoree you're heading to some made-up celebration.
- Instead of bringing the honoree to the surprise party, bring the surprise party to the honoree. Have guests first meet at your house. Then gather the food, gifts, decorations, and other supplies and travel to the honoree's house as a group. (See "Birthday-Party-in-a-Box" on page 130.)
- Make sure you write "Shh! It's a Surprise!" prominently on invitations. For extra insurance, call guests before sending invitations and give them a heads-up.
- Ask guests not to park their cars near the party site. Many a surprise has been spoiled when an honoree recognized friends' and relatives' cars. If this happens, don't be disappointed. The honoree will still enjoy hearing guests shout "Surprise!"
- Videotape the presurprise activity, such as volunteers setting up decorations and the guests getting ready to surprise the honoree. The honoree will enjoy seeing how much thought and effort went into planning his or her surprise.
- Keep in mind that surprise parties aren't for everyone. Make sure the honoree would really enjoy one.

Charming First Birthday Parties

Baby's first birthday is one of the most memorable milestones for his or her parents, even though Baby probably won't remember the event. Parents often invite relatives and family friends to celebrate the occasion. Since Baby is the center of attention at this party, you'll naturally want to include him or her as much as possible. But remember Baby's attention span may be short, and he or she may not tolerate the excitement for long. So keep the guest list and party time short, let Baby nap if necessary, take lots of photos or videotape the celebration, and enjoy the party!

Most activities listed in this chapter are geared toward adults and older children, but young children shouldn't feel left out; they'll relish the fun, exciting atmosphere. Remember the little ones, however, when planning the décor and menu. Keep small objects and balloons out of reach. Babies and young children may have trouble digesting traditional birthday cake, so give them just a taste or serve them an unfrosted sponge or angel food cake. Or try these easy-on-the-tummy cake and frosting recipes:

Baby's First Birthday Cake

1 cup sugar
6 eggs, separated
3 tablespoons lemon juice
¼ teaspoon salt
1 cup flour, sifted

Preheat oven to 325°F. Sift and measure sugar. Pour into small bowl. In another bowl, beat egg yolks thoroughly, adding sugar a bit at a time. Beat in lemon juice. In another bowl, beat egg whites and sprinkle salt into them. Continue beating until egg whites form stiff peaks. Gently fold them into yolk mixture. Sift flour and fold into batter a spoonful at a time. Pour into ungreased angel food cake pan. Bake 1 hour or until done.

Frosting for Tiny Tummies

2 cups brown sugar
⅔ cup water
1 egg white
⅛ teaspoon salt
½ teaspoon vanilla

Dissolve brown sugar in water. Boil mixture in top of double boiler until it's 238°F on candy thermometer. In small bowl, whip egg white and salt until frothy. Pour brown sugar mixture slowly over egg white while beating. Continue to beat until mixture forms peaks. Stir in vanilla and spread mixture on cake.

Whatever cake you choose, don't forget to capture the moment when Baby takes that first messy bite! *Note:* If you'll be using a candle, first make a wish for Baby, blow out the candle, and remove it before placing the cake in front of Baby.

Baby Buggy Boogie

Have guests hoppin' at the Baby Buggy Boogie, a first birthday party filled with merry music and fun.

INVITATIONS

Use invitations shaped like baby buggies or 45-rpm records. On the inside write:

Take a Walk on the Fun Side
at the
Baby Buggy Boogie
Celebrating
[Name]'s First Birthday
on [Date] at [Time]
[Address]

Or consider these invitation designs:

- Enclose a baby bootie and a note inviting guests to "Shake Your Bootie at a Baby Sock Hop!"
- Glue a photo of the baby on the label of a 45-rpm record. Or glue on a replacement label that reads "Baby Buggy Boogie." Write party details on a replacement label glued on the back of the record.
- Design an invitation that fits in the front of a CD or cassette case.
- Write party details between the staffs on blank sheet-music paper. Add music notes.

Whichever invitation design you choose, include a note inviting guests to bring their favorite children's CDs or cassettes.

DÉCOR

- Hang a banner that reads "Baby Buggy Boogie." Post a "Baby Buggy Parking Area" sign and park a few buggies near it.
- Park buggies throughout the room. (Buy them at thrift shops or borrow them from friends.) Fill them with baby toys. Use a buggy to collect gifts.

- Ask someone to be the deejay and spin tunes from the CDs and cassettes brought by guests.
- Make Boogie Baby posters: Find posters and photos of pop music stars and album covers that feature musicians. Copy photos of the birthday baby and cut out the faces. Glue the cutouts over the faces on the posters, photos, and album covers and use to decorate the walls.
- Use a buggy to hold bottled drinks and hors d'oeuvres. To keep drinks and food cold, place an ice-filled baby bathtub or large plastic container inside the buggy.
- Use vinyl-record bowls: Preheat oven to 350°F. Set a metal bowl upside down on a baking sheet or in a cake pan. Place a 33⅓-rpm record on top of the bowl. Bake just a few minutes until the record forms to the sides of the bowl. *Caution:* Don't bake too long, or the record will melt completely. Bake in a well-ventilated area.
- Serve punch in baby bottles with straws.
- Make napkin rings by folding pairs of sunglasses around napkins or by pulling napkins through the holes of 45-rpm records. Use 33⅓-rpm records as place mats.
- Use children's record players, boom boxes, or toy buggies as centerpieces. Fill toy buggies with buffet food, utensils, or napkins.

THEME-INSPIRED ACTIVITIES

- Play What Children's Song Am I?: Write titles of children's songs on slips of paper and pin one to each player's back. Have players ask one another yes-or-no questions to figure out the song titles on their own backs.
- Hold a Baby Buggy Relay: Divide the players into two teams. The first players in line push an empty buggy to a goal line. There they fill their buggies with baby toys or other baby items before returning to the starting line. The next players in line then push the buggies to the goal line, empty them, and return to the starting line. Repeat until one of the teams completes the relay. Award prizes to the winning team.
- Have a Baby Bottle Scavenger Hunt: Divide the players into two teams and give each team a buggy. Players hunt for hidden baby bottles and put them in their teams' buggies. The team that finds the most bottles within an allotted time wins prizes.

- Have a Baby Ball Crawl: Write various dollar amounts, such as -$1, -$5, $1, $10, $25, on brightly colored balls. Line up the baby players, then let them race to the balls. If a baby grabs a ball with a positive number written on it, his or her parents win that dollar amount. If a baby grabs a ball with a negative number written on it, the parents pay that dollar amount to the birthday baby.
- Play songs on your stereo or on a karaoke machine to help singers serenade the birthday baby. Have guests vote on the best performance. Award a prize to the best performer.
- Play musical chairs. For a humorous twist, use child-size chairs and have only the adults play.

MENU IDEAS

There will be lots of activity at this party, so serve a light buffet of simple, easy-to-handle menu items such as:

- Assorted crackers and cheeses
- Star-shaped sandwiches: Use a cookie cutter to cut peanut-butter-and-jelly sandwiches into star shapes.
- Miniature pigs-in-a-blanket
- Popcorn and chips
- Miniature muffins
- Tea and coffee
- Pink punch with ice cubes or ice blocks containing edible flower petals

DESSERT IDEAS

- Baby buggy cake: Bake a round cake. Cool, then remove top quarter (right or left) to create buggy shape. Frost the buggy, then place 2 frosted cupcakes at bottom of cake for wheels. Use frosting to add lacelike trim, wheel spokes, and birthday wishes. Add licorice loop for buggy handle.
- Cookies shaped like baby buggies
- Record cake: Cover a round cake with chocolate frosting. Add a brightly colored circle of icing in the center for a label. Write "Baby Buggy Boogie" on the label.

- Baby buggy ice-cream cakes: Slice a round ½-gallon cardboard tub of ice cream into 3 disks of equal thickness. Remove top quarter (right or left) of each disk to create buggy shape. Remove cardboard. Press 2 cookies or round candies into bottom of buggy for wheels. *Note:* You'll need to work quickly so buggy doesn't melt and lose its shape.

PARTY FAVORS AND PRIZES

- Shake Your Bootie snack bag: Fill a plastic sandwich bag with cereal like Froot Loops or Cheerios. Tie with ribbon.
- Baby Buggy to Go: Gift-wrap a box of animal crackers and glue on a hood and set of wheels, both made of construction paper. Add a loop of ribbon for the handle.
- CD or cassette of popular children's songs
- Baby rattle or bottle with guest's name written on it with puffy paints

GIFT SUGGESTIONS

- Silver-plated baby buggy bank
- Toy baby buggy and doll
- Children's boom box or record player
- CDs or cassettes of popular children's songs

Cute as a Button!

This charming first birthday party celebrates Baby's cute-as-a-button personality.

INVITATIONS

Glue a photo of the baby and a button onto the front of a note card. On the inside write:

[He or She]'s a Year Old,
We Do Decree.
And Cute as a Button
[He or She] Is, You See!
Come Celebrate
[Name]'s
First Birthday
on [Date] at [Time]
[Address]

Or consider these invitation designs:

- Cut a 4-inch-diameter circle from poster board. Glue a photo of the baby onto the circle. Punch two small holes through the circle (one on each side of the photo) so it looks like a button. Thread thin ribbon through the holes and tie a bow. Write party details on the back.
- Write party details on a sheet of paper. Roll it into a scroll, tie it with ribbon, and stuff it and a button into a plastic baby bottle. Attach an address label to the bottle, then have your local post office determine how much postage is needed to mail this unusual package.
- Glue buttons onto a string of paper dolls. Write party details on the paper dolls.

Whichever invitation design you choose, include a note inviting guests to bring baby photos of themselves.

DÉCOR

- Sew buttons onto several long lengths of ribbon. Crisscross ribbons across tablecloths, using double-sided tape to secure them.

- Make buttoned-up napkin rings: For each, sew a button on one end of a short length of wide ribbon. Slit a buttonhole in the other end of the ribbon.
- Make a button topiary for a centerpiece: Paint one large or two small Styrofoam balls green and glue on enough green buttons to cover the Styrofoam. Push a stick through the ball(s) for the trunk. Insert the trunk into a flowerpot or basket filled with floral foam and covered with florist's grass. Wind ribbon around the trunk and tie a bow at the top of the trunk.
- Or make a baby face topiary: Follow the directions above but replace the Styrofoam balls with double-sided baby face photos. To make, enlarge a photo of the birthday baby's face and make several copies. Glue two copies back-to-back and trim into a circle. Glue buttons around the photos and onto the base.
- Glue buttons all over the outside of a basket. Fill it with small toys, wrapped gifts, fruit, flowers, or balloons and use as a centerpiece.
- Use photos of the birthday baby in button-trimmed frames as centerpieces.

- Fill the bottoms of small clear jars with buttons. Set tea lights on top of the buttons. Place the jars on tables out of children's reach.
- Use cute-as-a-button dinner plates or saucers: Glue a photo of the birthday baby onto the center of a plate. Glue buttons around the photo. Place a clear glass plate on top. (This idea works best with a sit-down meal.)
- Display guests' baby photos on a table. Cover the table with the button-ribbon tablecloth described on page 13. Provide a basket of small, inexpensive frames for displaying unframed photos.

THEME-INSPIRED ACTIVITIES

- Play a baby-safe version of Button, Button, Where's the Button?: Players hunt for a button gift-wrapped in a small box.
- Fill a clear baby bottle with buttons and have players guess the number of buttons inside. Or fill a sock with buttons, tie it securely, and have players feel the sock and guess the number of buttons inside. Award a prize to the winner.

- Play Button Toss: Have players try to toss "buttons" (colored paper plates with drawn-on buttonholes) into a wagon or baby buggy.
- Hold a Button Up and Down Relay in which players must put on and take off a man's button-down shirt, buttoning and unbuttoning all the buttons while wearing mittens. Award a prize to the player who completes the task in the shortest time.

MENU IDEAS

- Nine-Patch Quilt Salad: Fill a square pan with lettuce. Make a 9-square grid on lettuce with strips of green pepper. Fill each square with toppings like shredded carrots, diced onions, shredded cheese, bacon bits, diced eggs, diced tomatoes, diced mushrooms, sunflower seeds, and diced cucumbers.
- Upside-Down Patty Cake: Preheat oven to 400°F. Place precooked sausage patties in the bottom of a greased baking dish. Make corn bread from scratch or from a mix. Pour batter over patties. Top with chili sauce. Bake 20–25 minutes. Turn cake upside down on platter and serve.
- Scrambled eggs with button mushrooms: Try the recipe below.

Scrambled Egg and Button Mushroom Bake

Sauce

4 slices bacon, diced
¼ cup margarine
1 4-ounce can button mushrooms
4 cups milk
½ cup flour

Egg Mixture

16 eggs
¼ teaspoon salt
1 cup evaporated milk
¼ cup margarine
1 4-ounce can button mushrooms

Preheat oven to 275°F. In saucepan, combine all sauce ingredients except flour over low heat. Cook until margarine is melted. Slowly stir in flour and cook over medium heat until mixture thickens. Set aside. In bowl, beat together all egg mixture ingredients except mushrooms. Pour mixture into different saucepan and cook, chopping up mixture as it cooks. (*Note:* Mixture should be very moist; do not overcook.) Grease 9-by-14-by-2-inch baking dish and alternate pouring layers of egg mixture and sauce mixture in it. Top with button mushrooms. Cover and bake 1 hour. Serves 12.

- Button-Fruit Trifle: In a clear trifle bowl, alternate layering button-size fruit (such as seedless red or green grapes, sliced strawberries, and sliced kiwi fruit) and miniature marshmallows. Just before serving, top with 24 ounces lemon yogurt combined with ½ cup honey and ⅓ cup pineapple juice.

- Button Pancakes: Make pancake batter from a recipe or mix. Add two raisins to each silver-dollar-size pancake as it cooks. Prepare beforehand and reheat just before serving.
- Champagne with strawberry buttons (strawberries sliced into circles)

DESSERT IDEAS

- Cake with a photo of the birthday baby's face transferred onto it and decorated with the message "Cute as a Button"
- Button-size cookies: Cut sugar or butter cookie dough into circles using a bottle cap. Poke two holes in the center of each cookie with toothpick before baking. Or cut cookie dough into circles with an upside-down 12-ounce tumbler. Spread jelly on one cookie and place another cookie on top. Gently press the layers together with upside-down 8-ounce tumbler. Poke 4 buttonholes in cookie with end of small paintbrush handle. Before baking, paint cookies with mixture of 1 egg yolk, ½ teaspoon water, and tiny amount of paste food coloring. Bake according to cookie recipe.
- Ice-cream buttons: Scoop small balls of different-colored ice cream using a melon baller. Place balls on baking sheet and freeze. Slightly flatten each ball with back of spatula. Poke 2 buttonholes in each ball with toothpick. Refreeze before transferring to dessert bowls.

PARTY FAVORS AND PRIZES

- Instant snapshot of guest holding the baby, placed in button-trimmed frame
- Button-trimmed photo on china saucer (See Décor.)
- Button cookies in a cellophane bag tied with ribbon
- Prize ribbon decorated with large buttons

GIFT SUGGESTIONS

- Gift certificate to a photography studio
- Cute outfit with button accents
- Baby toys
- Quilted photo album or scrapbook, decorated with buttons
- Children's "dress me" book, showing laces, zippers, and buttons

Teddy Bear Picnic

Teddy bears are favorite toys of the young and young at heart. Why not invite guests and their teddy bears to a Teddy Bear Picnic for Baby's first birthday?

INVITATIONS

Use invitations with a teddy bear motif. On the inside write:

You're Invited
to a Teddy Bear Picnic
for the
First Birthday
of Our Little Bear, [Name],
on [Date] at [Time]
[Address]

Or consider these invitation designs:

- Send the invitation in a small basket wrapped in a red-and-white-checked napkin. Or tie the invitation to a small teddy bear. (Inexpensive baskets and teddy bears are available at craft supply stores.)
- Attach the invitation to a jar of honey. Or glue the invitation over the label on a jar of honey.

Whichever invitation design you choose, include a note inviting guests to bring their favorite teddy bears.

DÉCOR

Hold the picnic in your yard or at a park, if weather permits. Or have a picnic indoors.

- Cover picnic tables with red-and-white-checked tablecloths or fabric with a teddy bear design. Or spread heavy blankets on the ground and lay the cloths over them. For an indoor picnic, spread the cloths on the floor.
- Play "Teddy Bear's Picnic" by Gary Rosen in the background.
- Have someone in a teddy bear costume greet guests with welcoming bear hugs.

- Use teddy bears as centerpieces. Accent them with picnic baskets.
- Set teddy bears on extra chairs at the table. Or set them at a small "bears only" table.
- Set up a Teddy Bear Corner under a tree for storytime. Hang colorful balloons, streamers, kites, and umbrellas from branches. If indoors, use a corner of the party room and hang the decorations from the ceiling.

THEME-INSPIRED ACTIVITIES

- Play Teddy Bear Who Am I?: Write the names of famous bears, such as Winnie-the-Pooh and Smokey Bear, on slips of paper. Pin one onto each player's back. Have players ask one another yes-or-no questions to figure out the names of the bears on their own backs.
- Play Teddy Bear Toss: Have players try to toss teddy bears into a large picnic basket or wicker laundry basket. The player who tosses the most bears into the basket wins a prize.
- Have a teddy bear pageant: Display the teddy bears brought by guests. Have guests vote which bear is Best Dressed, Most Loved (that is, tattered), and so on.
- Hire a storyteller to entertain the children (and adults) with bear stories like *Goldilocks and the Three Bears* at Teddy Bear Corner. (See Décor.)
- Play Musical Teddy Bears: Instead of removing a chair, set a teddy bear on it. Players can't sit on chairs with bears.
- Have a Brown Bear Hunt: Hide different-colored teddy bears throughout the party room. Award a prize to the player who finds the brown bear.
- Hold a honey tasting: Provide jars of honey in different flavors.

MENU IDEAS

- Teddy bear sandwiches: Cut peanut-butter-and-honey sandwiches into bear shapes with a cookie cutter.
- Porridge soup: Set a "Porridge" sign next to a crock of potato soup. Serve with brown bread and berries.

- Variety of fruits speared with toothpicks
- Bear claws or honey doughnuts
- Ants on a log: Spread celery sticks with peanut butter and top with raisins.
- Hunny Pot Punch: Add ⅔ cup honey to your favorite punch recipe. Pour punch into a large ceramic crock or cookie jar painted with word "HUNNY."

DESSERT IDEAS

- Cupcakes decorated to look like teddy bears or cookies shaped like teddy bears
- Pound cake brushed with honey and garnished with berries
- Teddy bear ice-cream scoops: Scoop ice cream into cupcake liners. Add cookie halves for ears, chocolate chips for eyes, and cherry halves for noses.
- Berries and ice cream
- Ice-cream treats for tots: In small bowl, mix together ½ can sweetened condensed milk with 1½ tablespoons cocoa and ½ cup whole milk. Freeze 2 hours. Beat with electric mixer. Pour into 3-ounce paper cups. Freeze 2–4 hours.

PARTY FAVORS AND PRIZES

- Jar of honey: Fill baby food jar with honey and cover lid with red-and-white-checked cloth. Tie with red ribbon. Add a note that reads "Hope the party was sweeter than honey!"
- Bit-O-Honey candy bar wrapped with ribbon
- Small teddy bear holding a tiny basket
- Teddy bear book

GIFT SUGGESTIONS

- Plush teddy bears
- Toy picnic basket tea set
- *Teddy Bear's Picnic* CD or cassette by Gary Rosen
- Clothing or toys with teddy bear designs

ABC Birthday Party

Planning this adorable first birthday party is as easy as ABC!

INVITATIONS

Use invitations with an alphabet motif. On the inside write:

"A" [He or She]'s Just Adorable;
"B" [He or She]'s So Beautiful;
"C" [He or She]'s a Cutie Full of Charm...
Join the ABC Birthday Fun
in Honor of
[Name]'s First Birthday
on [Date] at [Time]
[Address]

Or consider these invitation designs:

- Attach the invitation to a small ABC book.
- Attach an alphabet block to the invitation. Or use the block pattern on page 194 and trace the shape on cardstock. Write party details on the sides of the block. Fold into a block, tie with ribbon, and hand-deliver. Or leave the invitation flat and mail.

Whichever invitation design you choose, include a sheet of paper with an alphabet letter written on it and invite each guest to write a birthday wish inspired by the letter for Baby's scrapbook.

DÉCOR

- Tape letter cutouts spelling "Happy Birthday" to the front door. Cover the walls with letter cutouts.
- Gift-wrap large boxes with newsprint and write a letter on each side. Stack them around the room and top each stack with a bow.
- Build an alphabet block tower or place blocks in a basket. Use as a centerpiece.
- Label each guest's plastic cup with his or her first initial.
- Set a loot bag (lunch bag with a crayon letter drawn on) at each place setting.

THEME-INSPIRED ACTIVITIES

- Set out Scrabble and Boggle games for guests to play. For added fun, use alphabet blocks as playing pieces.
- Have a contest to see who can build the tallest alphabet block tower.
- Hide several alphabet blocks around the room. Have guests hunt for the blocks that spell the birthday baby's name. The first player to spell the name wins a prize.
- Provide pencils and note pads for players. Have them write down the names of guests or the months in alphabetical order. The first player to finish wins a prize.

MENU IDEAS

Serve a menu consisting of items that begin with the letters of the baby's first name. For example, Jesse's menu could be Jell-O salad, English muffins, shrimp scampi, steamed vegetables, and Edam cheese with fruit. Other ABC menu ideas include:

- Alphabet soup, ABC sandwiches (cut with alphabet cookie cutters), and ABC fruit (apples, bananas, and cherries)
- BLT (bacon, lettuce, and tomato) sandwiches and BLA (bacon, lettuce, and avocado) salad
- Alphabet cereal, ABC-branded toast (press alphabet cookie cutters halfway through bread before toasting), and ABC fruit
- Alphabet pancakes (pour pancake batter into metal cookie cutters set on a hot skillet), sausage, and eggs

DESSERT IDEAS

- Alphabet block cake: With frosting, draw a grid on a sheet cake. Write an alphabet letter inside each square.
- 3D alphabet block cake: Bake four 8-by-8-inch cakes. Cool. Place one cake on a platter and frost the top. Stack a second cake on the first one and frost its top. Continue stacking cakes in this way to make a cube-shaped four-layer cake. Frost the sides of the cube,

then decorate each side and the top with a letter. To serve, cut the cake layer by layer.

- Petits fours decorated to look like alphabet blocks

PARTY FAVORS AND PRIZES

- Box of alphabet cereal or can of alphabet soup trimmed with prize ribbons
- Alphabet block glued to a bag of candy or box of alphabet cereal tied with ribbon
- Photo of the birthday baby in a frame trimmed with glued-on alphabet blocks

GIFT SUGGESTIONS

- Alphabet blocks
- Toys decorated with alphabet letters
- Clothes with alphabet designs
- Alphabet books

Fairy-Tale Fifteenth Birthdays: *Quinceañeras*

In Latino cultures, a girl's fifteenth birthday marks her passage from childhood to adulthood. Many Latinas commemorate this milestone with a *quinceañera,* an elaborate celebration that can strengthen family and community ties, instill cultural pride, and renew religious beliefs.

The celebration can take years to plan. Securing a reception hall and church (if a church service is planned), assembling a guest list, choosing invitations, musicians, and choreographers, and so on can require a lot of patience and dedication. But for many, it's worth the effort. The birthday girl, *la quinceañera,* is truly a princess for a day. Traditionally, she wears a beautiful, full-skirted ball gown and may have a court of honor of up to fourteen couples of boys and girls to attend her at her ball, the quinceañera reception.

The quinceañera reception consists of five main parts: the introduction of the court of honor, the presentation of la quinceañera, the choreography, the *brindis* (toast), and the thank-you. Other customs, such as the honoree's changing her flats for high heels, being crowned with a tiara, waltzing with her father, and opening the five traditional gifts can also occur during the reception. A buffet or sit-down dinner is served and an elaborate multitiered cake is presented. Most receptions end with a dance. To learn more about quinceañera customs, read *Quinceañera!* by Michele Salcedo (Henry Holt, 1997).

Quinceañera receptions often follow a theme that reflects the honoree's interests, hobbies, favorite color or flower, and so on. Fantasy, storybook, or movie themes are also popular. Decorations and activities to enhance the theme can be simple or elaborate, depending on taste and budget. This chapter offers four charming themes for quinceañera receptions. Each can be customized to design the perfect party for la quinceañera.

Remember: These themes aren't just for quinceañeras. A Butterfly Ball or a Tango Tea Dance can be an ideal party theme for any milestone birthday celebration, such as a traditional sweet sixteen party or even a not-so-traditional sixtieth birthday bash.

Butterfly Ball

Like a butterfly emerging from its cocoon, la quinceañera enters adulthood with grace at her Butterfly Ball.

INVITATIONS

Use formal invitations. On the inside write or engrave:

Happiness is as a butterfly which,
when pursued, is always beyond our grasp,
but which if you will sit down quietly,
may alight upon you.
—Nathaniel Hawthorne

I, [Name], Wish to Invite You
to a Special Celebration
Hosted by My Parents
in Honor of My Fifteenth Birthday
on [Date] at [Time]
[Address]

If a church service is planned, include the date and time of the service and the church address in the above invitation and add the following:

Butterfly Ball Immediately Following Service
[Site Name and Address]

If not, replace *Special Celebration* with *Butterfly Ball.*
Or consider these invitation designs:

- Have the envelope embossed with a butterfly design.
- Write party details on a string of paper butterflies.
- Use invitations with a butterfly motif. Enclose butterfly-shaped confetti.

DÉCOR

- Place the guest book on a table or stand decorated with ivy garlands and silk butterflies. Attach a small silk butterfly to a thin wire covered with ribbon and wrap the wire around the guest book pen. Decorate the stemware in this way, too.
- Hang large silk butterflies (available at party and craft stores) from the ceiling.
- Place several potted trees around the room. Hang silk butterflies from the branches.
- Decorate chair backs, the bar, and the floral arrangements with large and small silk butterflies.
- Use bright floral-print tablecloths and use bright floral arrangements as centerpieces.
- Set small butterfly nets next to floral centerpieces. Place votive candles in glass holders and then set the holders in the nets.
- Fold napkins into butterfly shapes.
- Attach a small silk butterfly to a novelty high-heel shoe. Set a place card on the shoe.
- Decorate the quinceañera doll (doll that's dressed identically to la quinceañera and is a symbol of her youth) all over with small silk butterflies and *capias* (traditional ribbon favors given to guests).

THEME-INSPIRED ACTIVITIES

- Hire someone to make wax molds of guests' hands. For a finishing touch, have a small silk butterfly added to make it look as if the hand has caught a butterfly.
- Have the choreographer include butterfly nets in the introduction of the court of honor. For example, the nets can be used in an adaptation of the Spanish folk dance "Waltz of the Broom." Two lines of dancers face each other, with one line having one more dancer than the other. This dancer promenades between the lines with a butterfly net in hand. At some point, he or she drops the butterfly net and grabs a partner. At this time, the rest of the dancers also grab partners. This will leave one partnerless dancer, who then picks up the butterfly net and continues the dance.

- Have the court of honor release live butterflies when la quinceañera is presented. (See Supplier Resource Directory for vendors.)
- Seat la quinceañera on a rattan peacock chair decorated with silk butterflies for when her father changes her flats to high heels. La quinceañera is then ready for her first grown-up waltz with her father.
- Hire a mariachi band to serenade la quinceañera.

MENU IDEAS

- Hors d'oeuvres served with butterfly cocktail picks
- *Ensalada mixta* (mixed salad greens): Decorate the handles of serving utensils by securing silk butterflies to pieces of wire covered with ribbon and wrapping the wire around the handles.
- Tortilla chips with guacamole and *pico de gallo*
- Monarch *mole poblano* (turkey slices served in a chocolate-based sauce): Use a cookie cutter to cut turkey slices into butterfly shapes.
- *Arroz* (rice) and *frijoles refritos* (refried beans)
- Margaritas

DESSERT IDEAS

Display a multitiered birthday cake covered with spun-sugar butterflies. Surround it with one of these butterfly accents:

- Large butterfly-shaped sugar cookies placed in cellophane bags and tied with pastel ribbons and butterfly ornaments
- Flan molded into a butterfly shape
- Butterfly-shaped *bizcochitos* (crisp cookies usually flavored with anise)

PARTY FAVORS AND PRIZES

- Pack of bright-colored-flower seeds
- Decorated bag filled with butterfly-shaped chocolates
- Butterfly-shaped guest soaps
- Butterfly hair ornaments

GIFT SUGGESTIONS

- Photo frame or album trimmed with glued-on silk butterflies
- Butterfly identification guide, photo book, or journal
- Butterfly-design jewelry
- Gift certificate to a greenhouse

Cinderella Ball

A beautiful ball gown, a sparkling tiara, and an attending court of honor... This enchanting Cinderella ball can be la quinceañera's fairy-tale dream come true!

INVITATIONS

Have the following invitation printed on parchment. Then roll it into a scroll and tie with a gold, tasseled cord.

Once upon a Time,
There Was a Little Girl Named [Name],
Who Dreamed of Becoming a Beautiful Princess.
One Day Her Fairy Godmother Granted Her Wish
with a Quinceañera.
The Honor of Your Presence Is Requested
at This Fairy-Tale-Come-True Celebration.
on [Date] at [Time]
[Address]

If a church service is planned, include the date and time of the service and the church address in the above invitation and add the following:

Cinderella Ball Immediately Following Service
[Site Name and Address]

If not, replace *Quinceañera* with *Cinderella Ball.*

Or consider these invitation designs:

- Enclose a wand and attach the invitation to a gold-painted miniature pumpkin.
- Write the party details on a sheet of paper. Glue it onto the inside cover of an inexpensive copy of *Cinderella*. Or design your own storybook using the above invitation as the story. Wrap a gold, tasseled cord around the spine.
- Attach the invitation to a novelty glass slipper enclosed in a gift box.

- Enclose a photo of la quinceañera as a small child and/or a copy of her quinceañera portrait.

DÉCOR

- Hang a castle and moat mural on the wall. Add turret props to each side of the mural.
- Roll a red carpet down the entryway. Have the *chambelanes* (boys in the court of honor) line up along each side of the carpet and raise shiny swords to make an arch through which guests enter the ball.
- Display a chronology of photos from la quinceañera's life, from baby photos to her formal quinceañera portrait.
- Create a haven for la quinceañera and her *chambelán de honor* (honor escort): Over a table set for two, decorate a gold-painted structure made of lightweight wrought iron or latticed wood. Decorate the haven with royal splendor, paying special attention to la quinceañera's "throne." Have a white-gloved waiter ready to serve la quinceañera. Flank the haven with decorated tables and chairs for the court of honor.
- Cover guest tables with floor-length white chiffon and accent them with velvet runners trimmed with gold cord and tassels. Cover chairs in gold lamé accented with gold lamé or velvet bows.
- Complete the Cinderella theme with one of these centerpiece and place-setting combinations:
    - Glass slipper placed on a satin pillow trimmed with gold cord and tassels; place cards attached to novelty glass slippers
    - Large pumpkin dusted with gold glitter; place cards attached to matching miniature pumpkins
    - Large copy of *Cinderella*; place cards attached to smaller copies of the book
    - Large crystal clock, set at 12:00; place cards attached to matching miniature clocks

THEME-INSPIRED ACTIVITIES

- Hire a harpist or a hammered-dulcimer player to greet guests with Renaissance music.
- Seat her on a velvet throne for when her father changes her flats to a pair of transparent high heels. Have a "fairy godmother" wave her wand and place a rhinestone tiara on la quinceañera's head.
- Have the choreographer stage a more elaborate rags-to-riches performance. For example, as the court of honor waltzes on the dance floor, la quinceañera wanders in dressed in tatters. The fairy godmother arrives and leads Cinderella behind a curtain. The curtains open to reveal Cinderella dressed in her ball gown and tiara.
- Have the wait staff bring in food on silver trays to majestic trumpet and clarion music.
- Have a Cinderella slipper contest: Have each *dama* (girl in the court of honor) remove her shoes. Line up all the shoes in random order. Seat the damas on a row of chairs. One at a time, have each chambelán pick a shoe and try to find its owner. Time how long it takes each chambelán to find his Cinderella fit. The quickest chambelán wins a prize.
- Provide la quinceañera with a ceramic slipper for the brindis.

MENU IDEAS

- *Lechón* (roast suckling pig)
- *Arroz con camarones* (shrimp and rice)
- *Serenata* (salt codfish salad)
- Flaming *pastel de mapueyes* (yam pie): Pour brandy over the pie and ignite.

DESSERT IDEAS

- Multitiered cake decorated with edible fourteen-carat gold foiling (Contact a baker or caterer.)
- Chocolate Cinderella slipper molds with chocolate mousse (See Supplier Resource Directory.)
- Ice cream topped with flaming cherries jubilee

PARTY FAVORS AND PRIZES

- Inexpensive copy of *Cinderella*
- Novelty glass slipper filled with candy and wrapped in tulle
- Cellophane bag of candy tied to a wand with ribbon
- Small box of gold-dusted chocolates

GIFT SUGGESTIONS

- Diamond watch or bracelet
- Birthstone jewelry in a velvet jewelry box
- Leather-bound copy of *Cinderella*
- Madame Alexander Cinderella "last" doll (doll symbolizes the last toy la quinceañera will receive in childhood)
- Gift certificate to a shoe store

Pretty-in-Pink Garden Party

The quinceañera will blossom at this garden party decorated in pink from top to bottom.

INVITATIONS

Use elegant pink invitations. On the inside write:

[Name(s) of Host(s)]
Request(s) the Pleasure of Your Company
at a Quinceañera
to Celebrate the Fifteenth Birthday
of [Name]
on [Date] at [Time]
[Address]

If a church service is planned, include the date and time of the service and the church address in the above invitation and add the following:

Pretty-in-Pink Garden Party Immediately Following Service
[Site Name and Address]

If not, replace *Quinceañera* with *Pretty-in-Pink Garden Party*. Or consider these invitation designs:

- Write party details on a gift card. Attach the card to a stick planted in the soil of a small potted plant with pink flowers. Or slip the invitation underneath a ribbon wrapped around the pot.
- Tie the invitation with pink ribbon to a straw hat decorated with flowers.

- Attach the invitation to a pink flower (real or silk).
- Tie the invitation with pink ribbon to a ladies' white dress glove.

DÉCOR

Hold the reception in a garden or create an indoor garden by placing several potted trees and pink-flowering plants around the room. Whether the party is held indoors or out, consider using these ideas to decorate:

- Drape long pink ribbons or streamers from tree branches. Hang straw hats by their pink ribbons from tree branches or on fences or walls.
- Set up a bench swing decorated with pink ribbons and floral garlands.
- Attach each place card to a pink-flower seed packet or a single pink flower.
- Use pink tablecloths. Cover white wooden chairs with white organza and tie with large pink sashes.
- Use pink garden flowers in terra cotta flowerpots as centerpieces. Or make pink floral topiaries. Or find vintage purses that will sit upright. Set each on a white lace doily. Place a pearl necklace, a pair of ladies' gloves, and a hankie inside the purse and arrange them so they drape over the edges.
- Use pretty hats as centerpieces. Or place arrangements of pink flowers in hatboxes and accent them with jewelry, gloves, scarves, and so on.
- Wrap a ladies' white glove around each napkin and secure with a brooch or pink ribbon.
- Place a small white gift box filled with pink candies and wrapped with pink ribbon on each guest's plate. Attach a place card to the bow.
- Section off a corner of the room with a white picket fence to create a special garden for the *padrinos* (the celebration's sponsors). Decorate the area with potted pink rose trees and hang placards that name each padrino.

THEME-INSPIRED ACTIVITIES

- Introduce the court of honor and present la quinceañera with *la marcha,* a traditional Mexican-American grand march. Have everyone but la quinceañera march into the party in a figure eight and make a receiving line for the presentation of la quinceañera. Give the damas pink parasols to twirl. Lower la quinceañera from the ceiling on an elaborately decorated bench swing. Or open pink organza curtains to reveal her on the swing.

- Seat la quinceañera on a decorated bench for when her father changes her flats to a pair of pink high heels. The two can then dance to "Waltz of the Flowers" by Tchaikovsky.
- Invite guests to participate in a special Mexican hat dance. Instead of using sombreros, use wide-brimmed straw hats with pink bows.
- In a ceremony to thank the padrinos, have la quinceañera pick pink roses from the padrino garden (see Décor) and present one to each padrino.

MENU IDEAS

- Pink shrimp cocktails served in terra cotta flowerpots
- Stuffed pink tulips: Remove the insides of tulip blooms. Wash and air-dry the petals. Fill each with egg salad. (Petals are edible.)
- Basket of flower-shaped crudités
- Pea pods filled with salmon mousse
- Miniature prime rib sandwiches on rolls
- Spanish rice garnished with tiny pink carnation blooms
- Pink lemonade and pink champagne

DESSERT IDEAS

- Multitiered cake with pink frosting and designed with a champagne fountain or bridge
- Pink meringue swans
- Large sugar cookies decorated with flower designs
- Pink cotton candy: Rent a cotton candy machine and place it on a garden cart.

PARTY FAVORS AND PRIZES

- *Bonbonière* (candy box) of pink candied almonds: Place nuts on lace handkerchiefs. Gather ends and tie with pink ribbon.
- Pink flower-shaped soaps
- Pink rose or other pink flower
- Starched crocheted lace fan or high-heel shoe, tied with pink ribbon

GIFT SUGGESTIONS

- Pink pearl or pink topaz necklace or earrings
- Evening purse filled with a gift certificate or check
- CD of a favorite artist, wrapped in pink paper

Tango Tea Dance

Popular near the end of World War I at the Waldorf Hotel in London, the tango tea combines the sophistication of an afternoon tea with the passion of the tango. A Tango Tea Dance is sure to lend excitement and intrigue to any quinceañera!

INVITATIONS

Use formal invitations with red and black accents. On the inside write:

[Name(s) of Host(s)]
Request(s) the Pleasure of Your Company
at a Fifteenth Birthday Celebration
in Honor of
la Quinceañera, Miss [Full Name]
[Date]
at [Time]
[Address]

If a church service is planned, include the date and time of the service and the church address in the above invitation and add the following:

Tango Tea Dance Immediately Following Service
[Site Name and Address]

If not, replace *Fifteenth Birthday Celebration* with *Tango Tea Dance*. Or consider these invitation designs:

- Enclose a red rose (real or silk).
- Use invitations shaped like teacups.
- Attach the invitation to a tea bag.
- Write party details between the staffs on blank sheet-music paper. Add music notes. Title the invitation "Quinceañera Tango Tea." Roll it into a scroll, tie it with black ribbon, and slip a red rose under the bow.

DÉCOR

Hold this party in an elegant hotel ballroom or create your own ballroom.

- Set potted palms around the room.
- String lights around railings and walls.
- Greet guests with a string quartet playing boleros and tangos.
- Place seating assignments on china teacup-and-saucer sets. Display the sets on a table near the entrance.
- Set tables for two or four around the dance floor. Cover them with white linens and use matching napkins. Use small table lamps or candles.
- Choose from these centerpiece ideas:
  - Arrangement of fifteen red roses
  - Red rose arrangement in a teapot, silver sugar bowl, or tea service
  - Teapot covered with glued-on red rose blooms
  - Poster board silhouette cutout of tango dancers

- Have a white-gloved wait staff serve beverages from trolleys and food from tiered silver trays. Or cover a buffet table with white linen or lace and trim it with rose garlands. Have tea and coffee services set at each end of the buffet.
- Attach a red rose to each place card or place one on each napkin.

THEME-INSPIRED ACTIVITIES

- Have the choreographer plan several tango numbers for the introduction of the court of honor and the presentation of la quinceañera. Have each dama give la quinceañera a red rose. Or present la quinceañera by having her pop out of a large teapot or gift-box prop.
- Seat la quinceañera on a red velvet chair or love seat for when her father changes her flats to high heels. Then she and her father can dance the tango or a traditional waltz.
- Let everyone dance the tango. Hire an instructor to teach guests the dance.

- Hold a birthday-wish ceremony: Have the damas gather around the cake table. Give each a white taper candle in a silver or brass candlestick. If there are fewer than fourteen damas, give enough candles to female family members to make up the difference. Place a fifteenth candle on the cake table. Let la quinceañera blow out each candle and make a wish. She makes her last wish on the candle placed on the cake table.

MENU IDEAS

- Hors d'oeuvres: miniature chicken flautas (deep-fried tortilla rolls with filling), spicy chicken wings, *carnitas* (chunks of seasoned braised pork), fruit skewers, and so on
- English tea sandwiches: smoked salmon pinwheels, cucumber sandwiches, watercress sandwiches, egg salad sandwiches, and so on
- Quiches: quiche Lorraine, mushroom quiche, broccoli quiche, and so on
- Scones and crumpets served with Devonshire cream, lemon curd, and fruit jams
- Variety of hot teas, coffee, Mexican hot chocolate, and lemonade
- Kir royales, champagne, or tango cocktails (See recipe below.)

Tango Cocktail

½ ounce orange juice
½ ounce dry vermouth
½ ounce sweet vermouth
1 ounce dry gin
½ teaspoon Curacao

Shake well with cracked ice and pour into small cocktail glasses.

DESSERT IDEAS

Have a baker make a multitiered cake out of several teacakes, such as Victoria sponge cake, gingerbread cake, and so on. Have him or her construct a punch or champagne fountain inside the cake and place a teapot-shaped cake on top, tilting it so it looks as if punch or champagne is pouring out of it. Or choose from these desserts:

- Cake decorated with black lace Spanish fans and red roses.
- Fried ice cream

- Variety of tea cookies and desserts, such as madeleines, macaroons, jam tarts, anise cakes, and Mexican wedding cakes

PARTY FAVORS AND PRIZES

- Chocolate roses
- Potpourri teaspoon: Fill the bowl of a silver teaspoon with potpourri. Wrap the bowl in tulle and tie with ribbon.
- Wrapped box or tin of tea

GIFT SUGGESTIONS

- Trip to the Waldorf Hotel in London or to the birthplace of the tango, Argentina
- Stereo and collection of CDs or cassettes, featuring tangos, mambos, and so on
- Charm bracelet with a Tango Tea medallion or ring engraved with "15 *años* [years]"
- Tango lessons

Sensational Sixteenth Birthday Parties

It used to be turning sweet sixteen required having a pink and frilly affair where a girl could be a princess for a day. Consequently, the traditional sixteenth birthday party focused more on feminine interests than on any other interests a young woman or young man might have had.

For today's teens, however, turning sixteen means driver's licenses, dating, part-time jobs, and other new, exciting adventures and responsibilities. And traditional parties are often too sweet and sugary to celebrate this milestone accordingly. Contemporary parties focus on current trends and on the teen's interests.

This chapter offers party themes for music, car, science fiction, and sports enthusiasts, but don't forget that it's important to tailor the celebration to fit the honoree's personality. If your teen dreams of a traditional sweet sixteen party, see Fairy-Tale Fifteenth Birthdays: *Quinceañeras* for some sweet ideas. Or leaf through the other chapters to find the perfect party theme for your teen.

Car-Crazy Celebration

For many teens, the best thing about turning sixteen is being able to get their driver's licenses. So host a birthday party that drives this point home!

INVITATIONS

Use invitations with a car motif. On the inside write:

You're Invited to
a Car-Crazy Celebration for
[Name]'s 16th Birthday!
Cruise to [Address]
on [Date] at [Time].

Or consider these invitation designs:

- Write party details on the back of a poster board cutout of a license plate. Use the honoree's name as the plate "number."
- Write party details on a blank bumper sticker.
- Attach the invitation to a key chain.
- Glue the invitation onto a road map.

Whichever invitation design you choose, include a numbered key. Ask guests to bring the keys to the party.

DÉCOR

- Tie balloons onto the radio antennas of a few cars and park them near the front walk. Attach oversized "Happy 16th Birthday, [Name]!" bumper stickers (cut from poster board) to the bumpers.
- Tape posters of luxury cars and old license plates to the walls. Design and cut out different road signs from poster board and tape them to the walls.

- Make traffic lights: Blow up red, yellow, and green balloons. For each traffic light, place one balloon of each color (red on top, yellow in the middle, green on bottom) inside a rectangular cardboard frame.
- Use car-related items as centerpieces, such as bottles of motor oil, jugs of windshield fluid, ice scrapers, and so on. Tie ribbons and balloons to each item.
- Use novelty key rings as napkin rings.
- Serve beverages in travel mugs.

THEME-INSPIRED ACTIVITIES

- Hold a key drawing: On slips of paper, write the numbers written on the keys sent with the invitations. Award prizes to guests with the numbered keys that match the numbers drawn.
- Rent car-theme video games.
- Drive guests to an amusement park that offers bumpers cars and go-carts so everyone can drive a "car."
- Leave a few remote-control cars in the party area for guests to race.
- Play Name That Car Tune: Gather CDs or cassettes featuring car-theme songs, such as "Drive My Car" by the Beatles. Divide players into two teams. Have a member from each team listen to the first song. The first to identify the song title and artist or group—without help from the teams—wins a point for his or her team. Repeat with a new song and new players. The team with the most points wins a prize.

MENU IDEAS

- Grilled hot dogs and hamburgers
- Race car sandwiches: Use toothpicks to attach cucumber slices (wheels) to submarine sandwiches.
- Pizza
- Veggies and dip
- Cans or bottles of soda and water

DESSERT IDEAS

- Cake shaped and decorated to look like a car
- Driver's license cake: Have the baker decorate a sheet cake to look like a driver's license, transferring a photo of the honoree onto the cake.
- Tire cakes: Make a jellyroll using devil's food cake and whipped cream. Slice to make circles.
- Rocky road ice cream

PARTY FAVORS AND PRIZES

- Novelty key chain or plastic frame key chain with an instant snapshot of the guest and honoree
- Fun bumper sticker
- Toy car

GIFT SUGGESTIONS

A new car is every sixteen-year-old's dream gift, but here are some great substitutes if a new car just isn't in the budget:

- Gift certificate to a music store (for tunes to play in the family car)
- Key chain engraved with the number 16 and a gas station gift certificate
- Toy car and "gas" money
- Car-theme video games

Music Video Madness

Lights! Camera! Action! Host a sixteenth birthday party that lets guests be music video stars for a night.

INVITATIONS

Use invitations with a rock 'n' roll motif. On the inside write:

You're Invited
to Star with [Name]
in a
"[Honoree's first initial]"TV 16th Birthday Music Video!
Filming Begins at [Time] on [Day]
at [Address]

Or consider these invitation designs:

- Laminate the invitation, punch a hole in a corner, and thread a necklace-length ribbon through it. Write "VIP" on the envelope with a gold-ink pen and tie gold or black ribbon around it.
- Write a guest's name on the envelope, draw a gold star around the name, and seal the envelope with wax. Enclose this envelope inside another.
- Glue the invitation onto the cover of *Spin* or *Rolling Stone.*
- Slip the invitation into an empty CD case.

Whichever invitation design you choose, include a note inviting guests to bring their favorite CDs or cassettes.

DÉCOR

- Rent spotlights and position them to shine on your front door.
- Decorate a dance area with metallic streamers and Mylar balloons. Cover the dance floor with metallic confetti. Plug in strobe lights and set up a stereo system with lots of bass.
- Recruit a couple of volunteers to record candid party moments on video cameras. Edit the tapes later for a great memento for the honoree.

- Set up a few TVs around the party room and turn them to a music video station.
- Place lounge chairs and director's chairs around the room. Set a TV tray near each one.

THEME-INSPIRED ACTIVITIES

- Have a karaoke contest: For the first round, players choose the songs they wish to perform. A panel (selected beforehand) judges the performances and gives each a score from one to ten. For the second round, write song titles on slips of paper and put them in a bowl. Each player draws a slip and performs the song written on it. The panel judges this performance, and the player with the highest combined score wins a prize.
- Play Name That Tune Charades: Write popular song titles on slips of paper. Divide the players into two teams. Have one player draw a slip and act out the song title. If his or her team can't guess the song title within an allotted time, a member of the other team draws a slip to act out. If a team guesses correctly, it gets a point. The team with the most points wins prizes.
- Play Make a Music Video: Have the guests divide into teams. Give each team a boom box and a video camera. Tell teams they have an allotted time to choose a song from the CDs or cassettes they've brought, choreograph a routine, and record the performance. Place each team in a different well-lit room. When time is up, regroup and have the teams play the tapes of their performances. Let the guests decide the award each team receives, such as Best Choreography, Most Cheesy, and Best Lip-Synching.
- Hire a deejay (or recruit a volunteer) to spin tunes from the CDs and cassettes brought by guests. Let guests make use of the dance floor.

MENU IDEAS

- Submarine sandwiches
- Veggies and dip

- Potato chips, nuts, and popcorn
- Bottles or cans of soft drinks and water

DESSERT IDEAS

- Sheet cake decorated with a "[honoree's first initial]"TV logo
- M&M tin roof sundaes: Scoop vanilla ice cream into bowls and top with Peanut M&M's and chocolate sauce.
- "[Honoree's first initial]"TV ice-cream sandwiches: Using frosting, draw a "[honoree's first initial]"TV logo on a sugar cookie. Sandwich a scoop of ice cream between the decorated cookie and a plain one.

PARTY FAVORS AND PRIZES

- Empty videocassette case filled with candy
- Rock or pop single on CD or cassette
- Music videos on videocassette

GIFT SUGGESTIONS

- Collection of CDs featuring the latest MTV award winners
- Portable MiniDisc player
- Sixteen one-dollar bills in an empty CD case
- Hand-held TV

Party on Planet 16

Host a sci-fi birthday celebration at an out-of-this-world hot spot: Planet 16.

INVITATIONS

Use invitations with a galaxy motif. On the inside write:

You're Invited to a
Party on Planet 16
to Celebrate
[Name]'s 16th birthday
Star Date: [Date] at [Military time]
Sector: [Address]

Or consider these invitation designs:

- E-mail the invitation. Or if you're techno-savvy, post the invitation on a web site and mail or e-mail its address to guests.
- Save the invitation on a computer disk and mail it, along with a hard copy, in an envelope decorated with galaxy-theme stickers.
- Cut out a star from poster board. Cover it with aluminum foil and write party details on it with a marker.

DÉCOR

- Use black lights. If your budget allows, rent a fog machine to create an eerie atmosphere.
- Hang silver lamé curtains in doorways.
- Cut out star and planet shapes from poster board. Cover them with aluminum foil and hang them from the ceiling.
- Tape sci-fi posters on the walls.
- Pour water into various-size glass containers. Add a different color of food coloring to each one. Pour vegetable oil in the containers to create gooey bubbles. Set up small flashlights to shine on the containers.
- Paint galaxy shapes on tablecloths with glow-in-the-dark paint. Or cover tables with silver lamé.

- Write guests' names on computer disks and use as place cards.
- Post "XX-Files" and "XY-Files" signs on bathroom doors.

THEME-INSPIRED ACTIVITIES

- Provide virtual video games and hang an electronic dart board on the wall.
- If there's enough space to play, rent laser tag equipment.
- Transport the guests to a bowling alley to play Rocket Bowl, if available. Rocket Bowl (also known as Cosmic Bowling) is when a bowling alley turns down the lights, turns up the music, and illuminates the lanes with runway lights. If your local bowling alley doesn't offer Rocket Bowl, you can make your own Rocket Bowling alley. Set up plastic bowling pins on a smooth floor. Create lanes by laying down two strings of twinkling lights. Turn down the lights, turn up the music, and provide plastic bowling balls.
- Hire a deejay (or recruit a volunteer) to spin past and present dance tunes.

MENU IDEAS

- Wraps of Khan: Serve miniature tortillas with a variety of fillings, such as tofu, taco meat, and so on.
- Vulcan Nerve Pinches: Serve fried hot peppers stuffed with cheese.
- Blue and green tortilla chips with salsa
- Alien-green punch: Make lime Kool-Aid using lemon-lime soda instead of water.

DESSERT IDEAS

- Moon Cake: Frost a round cake with whipped cream and sprinkle shredded coconut on it. For a "green cheese" moon, tint the cake batter and whipped cream green.
- Simulated cake: Frost a cereal box and serve on a platter. Have a real cake ready to serve when the truth is learned.
- Starbucks Frappuccino clones: Combine ½ cup espresso, 2½ cups milk, ¼ cup sugar, 1 tablespoon dry pectin, and dash of cinnamon in a blender. Pour over ice.
- Alien-green milk shakes: Make milk shakes with mint–chocolate chip ice cream. Or add green food coloring to vanilla milk shakes.

PARTY FAVORS AND PRIZES

- Futuristic food bar: Wrap a king-size candy bar in aluminum foil and tie with metallic ribbon
- Alien or galaxy-theme key chain
- Videocassette of a sci-fi movie

GIFT SUGGESTIONS

- Virtual video game
- Astronomy software
- Video or DVD collection of sci-fi films, such as *Star Wars* and *The Matrix*
- Planet or constellation identification guide or a coffee-table book about the galaxy

Slam Dunk Celebration

This sporty sixteenth birthday party will score high with basketball-loving teens.

INVITATIONS

Make ticket invitations: Cut out 1-by-3-inch rectangles from poster board. On each write:

Here's Your Ticket to a
Slam Dunk Celebration:
Cheer on [Name]
as [He or She] Scores 16 Years!
Game Time: [Date and Time]
Location: [His or Her] Home Court,
[Address]

Or consider these invitation designs:

- Write party details on a poster board cutout of a basketball. Enclose basketball-design confetti.
- Attach the invitation to a miniature basketball. Or write party details on an inflatable plastic basketball.
- Copy a photo of the honoree in a basketball jersey and write the party details below the photo.
- Write party details on a high-top or write them on a cardstock postcard attached to the sneaker. Hand-deliver or mail (see page 2).

Whichever invitation design you choose, invite guests to come wearing basketball sneakers.

DÉCOR

Hold the party on a school, community, or professional basketball court. Or create your own basketball court:

- Mount a basketball hoop at each end of the party room.
- Use orange and black tablecloths.

- Choose centerpieces like:
  - Plush toys of a WNBA, NBA, or college basketball team mascot
  - Wheaties cereal boxes decorated with photos of the honoree
  - Small trophies
- Make place cards by writing guests' names on:
  - Miniature basketballs
  - Basketball trading cards
  - High-tops: Write "Michael Jordan," "Sheryl Swoopes," and other basketball stars' names on the sneakers and let guests choose their seats.

- Slip a plain basketball jersey over each chair back. Write "[Name]'s Slam Dunk Celebration" on each with puffy paints or a permanent marker.
- Tape WNBA, NBA, or college basketball team posters to the walls. For added fun, copy a photo of the honoree, cut out the outline of his or her face, and glue the cutout over a face on the poster.
- Post signs that read "Locker Rooms," "Concessions," Restrooms," "Press Box," and so on around the room.

THEME-INSPIRED ACTIVITIES

- Arrange a visit from a local professional or college basketball player to sign autographs, pose for photos, and just hang out with guests.
- Project *Space Jam, Hoop Dreams*, or another basketball movie on a wall.
- Let players play basketball or try these other basketball-theme games:
  - Basketball bowling: Use miniature basketballs to knock over plastic soda bottles.
  - Frisbee basketball: Toss Frisbees through basketball hoops.
  - Harlem Globetrotters relay: Divide the players into two teams. Have players brainstorm how teammates can pass the basketball to one another—overhead, around the back, through the legs, and so on. Let them decide the number of passing moves and in which order they should be passed. Then have the teams line up, give each a basketball, and let the teams race. Recruit referees to

make sure each team uses the correct passing moves in the correct order. The first team to finish the relay wins prizes.

- Rent basketball video games.

MENU IDEAS

- Hot dogs and pizza
- Nachos and warmed soft pretzels
- Popcorn
- Bottles of water and soda

DESSERT IDEAS

- Round cake decorated to look like a basketball
- Sugar cookies decorated to look like basketballs
- Hamburger cookies: Squeeze red frosting (ketchup), yellow frosting (mustard), and green frosting mixed with coconut (lettuce) onto a chocolate cookie. Sandwich the cookie between vanilla wafers. Brush the top wafer with egg white and sprinkle with sesame seeds.

PARTY FAVORS AND PRIZES

- Trophy cup filled with foil-wrapped chocolate basketballs
- Nerf miniature basketball and hoop
- Videotape of a basketball movie

GIFT SUGGESTIONS

- Tickets to WBNA, NBA, or college basketball game(s)
- Basketball and/or hoop
- WBNA, NBA, or college basketball team jersey, jacket, or cap
- Basketball merchandise or celebrity photo signed by a basketball star
- Subscription to *Sports Illustrated*

Terrific Twenty-First Birthday Celebrations

For many young adults, turning twenty-one is one of the most eagerly awaited events in their lives. At this age, they're considered full-fledged adults and must accept responsibility for their actions.

One way many celebrate this milestone is to hit the bars and nightclubs, with alcohol the obvious focus of the party. But not every new twenty-one-year-old drinks or wants his or her party to revolve around alcohol. This chapter offers themes for engaging and entertaining parties—a chauffeured club crawl, an elegant dinner, a disco party, and a beach party—that focus not on alcohol but on having a terrific time.

As always, if alcohol is involved in your celebration, be aware of how much guests (who are twenty-one or older, of course!) consume. And if guests do drink, please don't let them drive.

Chauffeured Club Crawl

At this progressive twenty-first birthday celebration, partygoers are chauffeured from club to club or from one fun destination to another. Use your vehicle—and friends' or family members' vehicles, if necessary—to transport the party. Or for a special touch, hire one or more chauffeured limousines to do the job in style.

INVITATIONS

Use invitations with a car motif. On the inside write:

You're Invited to a
Chauffeured Club Crawl
to Celebrate [Name]'s
21st Birthday.
Please Meet at [Address]
on [Date] at [Time] to Join
the Progressive Party.

Or choose one these invitation designs:

- Write party details on a cardstock postcard and decorate the back with car stickers.
- To entice guests, enclose a mysterious Club Crawl itinerary with the invitation. For example, it could read "*Club stop 1:* It's a secret! *Club stop 2:* We can't tell! *Club stop 3:* You'll have to wait and see!" and so on.
- Attach a miniature-car key chain to the invitation.
- Glue the invitation onto a road map.

Whichever invitation design you choose, ask the guests to bring their favorite CDs or cassettes.

DÉCOR

- If using personal vehicles, wash each one and clean the interior. Have drivers wear chauffeur formalwear. Attach balloons to the radio antennas and post signs that read "[Name]'s 21st Birthday Club Crawl" on the doors.

- Secure bunches of balloons inside the vehicles, taking care not to obstruct the driver's view.
- If guests don't have easy access to the vehicles' stereo systems, set a boom box in each vehicle so they can play the CDs and cassettes they've brought.
- Leave several disposable cameras in the vehicles for guests to snap photos of the party fun.

THEME-INSPIRED ACTIVITIES

Before the Club Crawl begins, have the honoree suggest a list of places to hit. The itinerary can change as the party progresses, but the drivers (especially limousine chauffeurs) may want to know roughly where they'll be driving and how long they'll be at each destination. While at the clubs, suggest that the guests:

- Have the deejay play a special tune for the honoree.
- Gather as many people as possible to help serenade the honoree.
- Get as many people as possible to dance with or give best wishes to the honoree.
- Pop a bottle of champagne or sparkling cider to toast the honoree.

While crawling from club to club may be the ticket to birthday fun for some, it may not be for others. If a club crawl isn't desirable or appropriate, have the honoree suggest some other destinations to visit and an itinerary to follow, such as the following:

1. Bowling alley or sports bar: Get the guests in a party mood with bowling, pool, darts, foosball, and so on.
2. Restaurant: Make reservations at the honoree's favorite restaurant. If you are picking up the check for all of the guests, consider pre-ordering a variety of appetizers and drinks instead of having the guests order full meals.
3. After-hours dance club: If there isn't an appropriate dance club in your area, decorate your garage or a room in your house to look like one. Clear a dance floor, plug in strobe lights, and use black

lights. Set up a stereo system with lots of bass and ask someone to spin the CDs and cassettes brought by the guests.

MENU IDEAS

In the vehicles, place coolers stocked with:

- Bags of pretzels and nuts
- Veggies and fruit
- Bottles of soft drinks, water, and juice

DESSERT IDEAS

At one of the crawl stops, serve:

- A cake (or sugar cookies) decorated to look like a limousine and with "[Name]'s 21st Birthday Club Crawl" written in frosting.
- Decorated cakes shaped in the numbers 2 and 1.
- Cupcakes, each served with a birthday candle.

PARTY FAVORS AND PRIZES

- Plastic photo-frame key chains with photos of guests: Take instant snapshots of everyone in the chauffeured vehicles. Trim the snapshots to fit into the frames.
- Decorated envelope of dollar bills to help pay for any cover charges

GIFT SUGGESTIONS

- Twenty-one CDs or cassettes of honoree's favorite artists, stacked and tied with ribbon
- Gift certificate to a music store
- Toy limousine attached to an envelope of "tip" money
- Passes to a favorite club
- Gift certificate to a gas station

Retro Disco Party

This retro disco celebration will get your guests groovin'!

INVITATIONS

Use smiley-face invitations. On the inside write:

Flash Back to the 1970s
at a
Retro Disco Party
for
[Name]'s
21st Birthday
on [Date] at [Time]
[Address]

Or consider these invitation designs:

- Pin a smiley-face button to the invitation. Or write party details with a marker on an inflated smiley-face balloon. Deflate it and mail in an envelope decorated with smiley-face stickers.
- Copy a photo of John Travolta striking his famous *Saturday Night Fever* disco pose, and glue it onto a note card. Write party details inside.
- Glue the invitation onto an 8-track cartridge (and maybe include a note explaining what it is!).

Whichever invitation design you choose, ask guests to wear bell-bottoms, hip-huggers, miniskirts, halters, platform shoes, Afro wigs, and so on. Also ask each to bring a CD or cassette of 1970s music to exchange.

DÉCOR

- Hang bead curtains in doorways.
- Hang a disco ball above the dance floor. String lights around the room and plug in strobe lights.

- Play disco tunes in the background.
- Cover tables with avocado, burnt sienna, and gold double-knit polyester fabric.
- Use lava lamps as centerpieces or room accents.
- Make a platform centerpiece: Tape together the sides of five 1970s album covers to make a cube. Set a pair of platform shoes on top.
- Paint guests' names on pet rocks and use as place cards.
- Pin smiley-face buttons onto napkins.

THEME-INSPIRED ACTIVITIES

- Do the CD Hustle: Gather players in a circle on the dance floor. Distribute the CDs or cassettes brought by guests. Start the music and have players keep passing the CDs or cassettes to the right. When the music stops, each player passes his or her CD or cassette to the player a designated number of players to the left, who then wins that CD or cassette.
- Play Name That 1970s Tune: Gather CDs of classic 1970s music. Divide the players into two teams. A member of a team listens to a few seconds of a song. He or she must then guess its title. If correct, his or her team wins a point. If incorrect, the other team has a chance to guess. If it guesses correctly, it gets a point and the next chance to guess. If it guesses incorrectly, the first team tries again with a new song. The team with the most points wins prizes.
- Play Smiley-Face Twister: Draw smiley-faces on the Twister circles.
- Have a disco dance contest: Teach the guests several disco dances, such as the Bump and the Electric Slide. Clear a dance floor and let the dancers compete. Have the guests vote for the best dancers.
- Have a 1970s karaoke or lip-synch contest. Videotape each contestant's performance and have guests vote for the best performer.

MENU IDEAS

- Potato chips, popcorn, and cheese-flavored snacks
- Pizza rolls
- Veggies and dip
- Fruit salad
- Soft drinks, beer, or wine coolers served in Tupperware tumblers

DESSERT IDEAS

- Ding Dongs, Ho Hos, Sno Balls, and Twinkies
- Cake decorated to look like a smiley face
- Brownies
- Rainbow sherbet

PARTY FAVORS AND PRIZES

- Mood ring
- Pet rock
- Smiley-face pin, jewelry, or beanbag toy
- CD or cassette of disco or 1970s music

GIFT SUGGESTIONS

- Bottle of champagne or sparkling cider decorated with smiley-face stickers
- Gift certificate to a music store
- CD or cassette collection of disco and 1970s music
- Lava lamp
- Beanbag chair

Dinner at '21'

Re-create the 1920s uptown elegance of New York's fabled '21' Club for a posh twenty-first birthday celebration.

INVITATIONS

For formal invitations, have the following details engraved in black ink on ecru or white letter sheets:

In Honor of
[Name],
[Name(s) of Host(s)]
Request(s) the Company of
[Hand-write guest's name]
for Cocktails and Dinner
[Day], [Date]
at [Hour]
'21' Club
[List party address in parentheses]
Black Tie Requested

For informal invitations, choose one of the following ideas:

- Write party details on a postcard featuring the real '21' Club.
- Tie together a playing card hand totaling twenty-one with ribbon and enclose in the invitation.
- Design a *New York Times* front page invitation: Find a front page of the *New York Times*. On a sheet of paper, write or type "[Honoree] Spotted at Posh '21'!" in big block letters. Trim the statement to fit over the newspaper's headline. Write party details on another sheet of paper and center it over the newspaper's text. Photocopy the invitation.

DÉCOR

- Roll a red carpet down the front walk and have a formally dressed doorperson greet guests.
- Design a mural of the '21' Club façade, including the famous jockey hitching posts, and hang it near the entrance of the party room.
- Play 1920s jazz tunes in the background.
- Let guests learn their seating assignments by giving each a brass money clip engraved with the number 21, with the seating assignment tucked inside. Or give each a hand of playing cards that add up to twenty-one. Stack and tie the cards with ribbon and write the seating assignment on the back of the bottom card.
- Use white linen tablecloths and fine china and crystal place settings. Place a globe-covered candle on each table. Use a floral arrangement or a single rose as a centerpiece.
- Attach place cards to cigars or long cigarette holders.
- Place a black or white balloon—filled with confetti, candy, and party favors—at each place setting.

THEME-INSPIRED ACTIVITIES

- Hire a flapper dance act to entertain the guests and teach them dances from the 1920s. Clear a dance floor and play 1920s dance music to let guests practice what they've learned.
- Have a 21/'21' trivia contest: Prepare a list of questions and answers about the honoree's history and the history of '21'. What was the honoree's first paying job? Where was the secret wine cellar located in '21'? Divide the guests into two teams. Ask one team a question. If the team can't answer, the other team can try. If neither team answers correctly, ask the next question. If a question about the honoree's history is asked of the team with the honoree, he or she is not allowed to help the team. Award a point for each correct answer. The team with the most points wins prizes.
- Stage a government sting: Arrange for a few volunteers dressed as Federal agents and police officers to barge into the party, confiscate the liquor, and round up the "suspects." As the authorities slap handcuffs on each suspect, take an instant snapshot of the moment and write "I was stung at [Name]'s '21' bash!" on it. Attach the snapshot to a pair of plastic handcuffs and give as a party favor.
- Hit a dance club after dinner and games.

MENU IDEAS

Serve a menu based on one served at the '21' Club, such as:

Appetizer
Maine Crab Cake
with Cucumber Salad and Curry-Carrot Sauce

Main Course
Hickory-Fired Filet Mignon
with Stone-Ground Corn and Chanterelles

Side Order
Potato Soufflés

Dessert
Whiskey-Scented Warm Chocolate Cake
with Caramel Ice Cream

- Create a menu based on celebrity '21' Club regulars. Find recipes to make your versions of dishes like Oysters Rockefeller, Ernest Hemingway Sea Bass, Cary Grant Eggplant Parmigiana, and a Donald Trump Golden Soufflé.
- Fill a claw foot bathtub with ice and bottles of hooch and giggle water (alcoholic beverages).

DESSERT IDEAS

- Cake decorated with the '21' Club logo
- Vanilla ice cream profiteroles with "21" written on them in chocolate sauce
- Your version of the Whiskey-Scented Warm Chocolate Cake with Caramel Ice Cream from the menu above
- 100 Grand candy bars served in cigar boxes

PARTY FAVORS AND PRIZES

- "Bootleg" bottle (liquor bottle) filled with candy
- Framed postcard of '21'
- Real, brass, or crystal apple engraved with the words (or attached to a note that reads) "[Name]'s Big Apple Night"

GIFT SUGGESTIONS

- Season or single tickets to a performing arts center
- Twenty-one one-dollar bills placed in cigar box
- Trip to the real '21' Club in New York City
- Formalwear for this or future posh parties
- CD or cassette collection of Broadway musical hits

Birthday Splash

Celebrate a beachside twenty-first birthday that will make a big splash with guests!

INVITATIONS

Use invitations with a beachside motif. On the inside write:

Join [Name] for Some
Fun in the Sun
at [His or Her] 21st Birthday Splash
on [Date] at [Time]
[Address]

Or consider these invitation designs:

- Enclose a drink umbrella or a small seashell.
- Write party details on the label on a bottle of suntan lotion.
- Attach the invitation to a pair of sunglasses, a roll of Lifesavers, or a plastic fish.
- Write party details on a sheet of paper, roll and tie it with ribbon, slip it into a bottle, and cork the bottle.
- Attach the invitation to a terry cloth hand towel or washcloth. Or write the party details on the towel or washcloth with a fabric pen.

Whichever invitation design you choose, invite guests to come dressed in beachwear and to bring their swimsuits if necessary.

DÉCOR

If possible, hold the party near a pool or on a beach. If not, bring the beach inside. Hang beach balls from the ceiling. Set out lawn chairs and prop up beach umbrellas. Tape posters of seaside locations to the walls. Whether the party is held indoors or out, consider using these ideas to decorate:

- Play calypso or beach-rock music, such as tunes by The Beach Boys, in the background.

- Swipe fluorescent zinc oxide on guests' noses at the door.
- Lay a surfboard across two sawhorses and use as a buffet table.
- Use patio tables with umbrellas. Cover tables with colorful beach towels or drape the towels over chair backs.
- Set votive candles in plastic sand pails filled with sand; use as centerpieces.
- Use terry cloth washcloths as napkins and make napkin rings by folding pairs of sunglasses around them.
- Use upside-down Frisbees as plates.
- For place cards, write guests' names on bottles of suntan lotion, plastic sand pails, or plastic shovels.

THEME-INSPIRED ACTIVITIES

- On a large piece of cardboard, draw a headless bodybuilder and beach bunny. Cut two head-size holes where the heads belong. Guests can stand behind the cardboard and put their heads through the holes for a great photo opportunity.
- Have a Beachcomber's Treasure Hunt: Fill a kiddie pool with sand. Bury several treasures in it, such as seashells, change, beads, crayons, costume jewelry, rubber ducks, plastic fish, and so on. Have guests dig for treasures for an allotted time. Afterward, post a sign that lists the treasures and their corresponding points. For example, a shell equals one point, a padlock equals twenty-five points, and so on. The player who finds treasures worth the most points wins a prize.
- Hold a limbo contest. Play Beach Blanket Twister.
- Hold a beach ball relay: Divide the players into two teams. The first players for each team hop to a specified location with a beach ball between their knees. At that location, the players each put on a pair of flippers and run the ball back to the starting line. The second players then put on the flippers and reverse the tasks.
- If the party is held near water, have guests play water sports like water volleyball, basketball, or football.
- Clear a dance floor for guests to do the Swim and other beach dances.

MENU IDEAS

- Deviled eggs garnished with drink umbrellas
- Clam chowder
- Grilled hamburgers, hot dogs, and bratwursts
- Flowerpot shish kebabs: Make a flowerpot grill by filling a flowerpot at least eleven inches tall with dirt or gravel to within five inches of the top. Cover the dirt or gravel with a circle of aluminum foil and add a layer of charcoal. Place a metal cooling rack across the top of the flowerpot. Stick bite-size chunks of meat and vegetables onto skewers, light the charcoal, and place the skewers on the rack. Grill until thoroughly cooked.
- Fish sandwiches
- Goldfish crackers served in sand pails
- Homemade wine coolers: Pour wine and fruit juice into a large galvanized tub. Add slices of fruit to garnish.
- Iced tea, lemonade, and bottles of soda, beer, and wine coolers

DESSERT IDEAS

- Sand pail cake: Cut a sheet cake into 1-inch cubes. Place alternate layers of cake cubes and pudding in plastic sand pails. Top with crushed graham crackers and garnish with chocolate shells. Use a plastic sand shovel to serve.
- Strawberry shortcakes, each decorated with a birthday candle
- Shark Bites: Make Berry Blue Jell-O. Pour into clear plastic cups and add Gummi fish before gelatin sets.
- S'mores: Sandwich a square of Hershey's milk chocolate and a freshly toasted marshmallow between two graham cracker squares.

PARTY FAVORS AND PRIZES

- Surfboard key chain
- Funky beach hat
- Seashell filled with potpourri and wrapped with tulle
- Bottle of bubbles
- Roll of Lifesavers

GIFT SUGGESTIONS

- Waterproof watch
- Pair of in-line skates
- Gift certificate for a new swimsuit
- Vacation to a beachside paradise
- Buried treasure: Place twenty-one one-dollar bills in a plastic sandwich bag, fill a plastic sand pail with candy, and bury the bag in the candy. Include a plastic shovel to help dig out the treasure.

Smashing Thirtieth Birthday Bashes

Some people think that when you reach thirty, everything goes downhill. Wrinkles, cellulite, love handles, potbellies—these are just some of the fears that plague twenty-something men and women as they approach this milestone. Many people also think turning thirty means putting career and family ahead of hedonistic pleasures. The age is supposedly a deathblow to good times.

But this milestone birthday needn't be troubled with such dramatic melancholy. Here are four themes for celebrations that poke fun at the doomsday perception of turning thirty.

Derby Day Party

This party pokes fun at the "ancient" thirty-year-old mare or stallion, combining the excitement of the Kentucky Derby, southern hospitality, and over-the-hill party antics.

INVITATIONS

Use invitations with a horse motif. On the inside write:

It's Time for a
Derby Day Party!
Place Your Bet
on the 30-Year-Old,
[Name], to Win
on [Date] at [Time]
[Address]

Or consider these invitation designs:

- Write party details on a mock racing form or tout sheet.
- Enclose a red rose (real or silk) to symbolize the Run for the Roses.
- Write party details on a poster board cutout of a rocking horse.
- Glue the invitation over the label on a miniature bottle of Kentucky bourbon.

DÉCOR

- Hang a banner that reads "Derby Day Party Starting Line" near the entrance. Post a sign that reads "Park Your Rocker Here" and park a few rocking chairs and rocking horses near it.
- Use blue tablecloths and use red rose or spring flower arrangements as centerpieces. Or make a centerpiece using an equestrian hat, riding crop, trophy cup, horse figurine, and framed photo of the honoree.
- Attach balloons with an over-the-hill motif to chair backs.
- Garnish plates with edible flower petals and scatter more petals over the table.
- Use mock racing forms and tout sheets as place cards.

THEME-INSPIRED ACTIVITIES

- Design racing forms, tout sheets, and Derby Day Party programs and give them to guests as they arrive. Guests can place their bets on the Derby Day races described below.
- Play Race to the Tables: Label each table by displaying a rocking horse cutout on each one. Write a different racehorse name, such as Lightning or Secretariat, on each cutout. For each place setting at each table, write the table's racehorse name on a slip of paper. Stuff each slip into a gray balloon. Inflate the balloons and set them on the floor along a wall. At your signal, have the guests race to the balloons, each stomp on one balloon, read the racehorse names on the slips inside, and race to their tables. Award prizes to the dinner partners who all reach their table first.
- Hold a three-legged race: Have players pair up and stand side by side. For each pair, tie one player's left leg to the other player's right leg. Line the pairs up at a starting line. At your signal, have them race around a track. The first pair to cross the finish line wins a prize.
- Have a Rocker Derby: Have players sit on rocking horses or in rocking chairs lined up at a starting line. At your signal, have them use their legs to rock or hop forward or push backward to the finish line. Award prizes for first, second, and third place winners.

- Rent horserace video games. Or head out to the racetrack if one is nearby.

MENU IDEAS

Serve a southern-style brunch: grilled ham, scrambled eggs with black-eyed peas, grits and redeye gravy, biscuits, and freshly squeezed orange juice. Or choose among these refreshments:

- Shredded beef brisket barbecue or grilled ham sandwiches
- Benedictine sandwiches: Combine grated cucumbers, onion, cream cheese, and mayonnaise. Spread on bread slices.
- Ham slices with prune sauce
- Prune muffins

- Mint juleps, served as guests arrive: Pour ⅓ cup mint julep syrup (see recipe below) and ¼ cup 100-proof Kentucky bourbon into frozen silver julep cups or tall glasses filled with crushed ice. Garnish with mint sprigs.

Mint Julep Syrup

1½ cups water
4 cups granulated sugar
1 bunch fresh mint sprigs

Combine water and sugar in pan and bring to a rolling boil. Simmer until syrupy. Cool. Pour into a jar, add mint sprigs, seal, and refrigerate overnight. Strain and discard mint. Mixture will keep for several weeks in refrigerator. Makes 12 juleps.

DESSERT IDEAS

- Coconut cake
- Bourbon pound cake
- Prune brownies: Substitute prune purée for butter in a brownie recipe.
- Prune ice cream: Mix sweetened puréed prunes and ice cream in a food processor and refreeze.
- Frosted prune cake (see recipes below):

Over-the-Hill Prune Cake

2 cups flour
¼ teaspoon salt
1 teaspoon baking soda
1 teaspoon cinnamon
¼ teaspoon nutmeg
⅓ cup butter
1 cup sugar
2 eggs
1 cup prune juice
1 cup chopped prunes

Preheat oven to 350°F. Sift flour, salt, soda, and spices in bowl and set aside. Cream butter and sugar and mix in eggs. Beat 3 minutes. While stirring, alternately add small amounts of prune juice and dry ingredients to butter mixture. Stir in chopped prunes. Pour into 2 greased and floured 9-inch round cake pans or one 9-by-13-inch pan. Bake 40–45 minutes. Cool, then frost.

Over-the-Hill Frosting

1 8-ounce package cream cheese
1 stick butter, softened
1 teaspoon vanilla
1 pound powdered sugar
10–12 prunes, dried and pitted

Cream first 4 ingredients until fluffy. Frost cake, then trim with prunes.

PARTY FAVORS AND PRIZES

- Old Kentucky Bourbon Chocolates, Derby Mints, Chocolate Thoroughbreds, or Old Fashion Pulled Creams wrapped in cellophane and tied with ribbon (See Supplier Resource Directory.)
- Kentucky Derby T-shirt (Or have special Derby Day T-shirts made.)
- Miniature bottle of Kentucky bourbon (Award a larger size bottle as a game prize.)
- Over-the-hill first-aid kit: gray-hair net, box of prunes, wrinkle patches (Band-Aids), and birthday-control pills (pill bottle filled with M&M's or jellybeans)

GIFT SUGGESTIONS

- Wood rocking chair
- Night out at a local horseracing track
- Thirty red roses in a silver trophy vase
- Box of Old Kentucky candies
- Bunch of balloons attached to a bottle of Geritol and a note offering to treat the "aging" honoree to lunch

Birthday Bird Bash

Turning thirty shouldn't ruffle the honoree's feathers. Celebrate this milestone with a bash sure to have guests flying high!

INVITATIONS

Use invitations with a bird motif. On the inside write:

Let [Name] Know
Turning Thirty
Is for the Birds!
Come to a
Birthday Bird Bash
on [Date] at [Time]
[Address]

Or consider these invitation designs:

- Use invitations with a sunflower-motif. Or attach the invitation to a silk sunflower or a packet of sunflower seeds.
- Write party details on a poster board cutout of a birdhouse.
- Attach the invitation to a pair of toy binoculars.
- Fold the invitation into an origami bird.

DÉCOR

Hold the party in a park or in your garden. Or create a garden indoors. For either location, consider using these ideas to decorate:

- Hang birdhouses from tree branches, the patio roof, or the ceiling. Post signs on the birdhouses that read "Turning 30 is for the birds!" and "Birds of a feather party together!"
- Use a birdbath to store gifts.
- Serve food in bird feeders and birdbaths placed on a buffet table.
- Use robin-redbreast-colored tablecloths and accent with robin's-egg-blue napkins. Surround each plate with florist's grass.

- Use birdhouses as centerpieces. Surround with florist's grass and sprinkle confetti and birdseed over them.
- Use small birdhouses, bird ornaments, toy binoculars, or packets of flower seed as place cards.
- Fold napkins into origami birds.
- Wrap ivy garland around napkins and place one on top of each water glass.

THEME-INSPIRED ACTIVITIES

- Play Feed the Birds: Hang doughnuts, each tied to string, from the ceiling. Tie players' hands behind their backs. Instruct players to eat their doughnuts without using their hands. The player who finishes his or her doughnut—and has the fewest crumbs on the floor—wins a prize.
- Play Drinking Bird: Have players sit at the table and tie their hands behind their backs. Pour martinis or daiquiris (alcoholic or virgin) into shallow, wide-mouthed glasses and add olives or cherries. Place a drink with a straw in front of each player. At your signal, players lean forward and bob for their olives or cherries. Once they've eaten these, they must suck the drink through the straw. Say "Stop!" every few seconds. Players must then stop bobbing or sucking and sit up. Repeat until a player has eaten the olive or cherry and sucked down his or her drink. Award a prize to that player.
- Have a bird-watching scavenger hunt: Divide the players into teams. Give each team a pair of binoculars, a bird identification guide, an instant camera, and a list of birds to find. Include other outdoor treasures to find if your neighborhood doesn't have a several species of birds. The first team to snap shots of all the items on the list wins prizes.
- Clear a dance floor and let guests shake their tail feathers. Be sure to include some bird tunes like "Rockin' Robin."

MENU IDEAS

- Garden salad
- Bird's nest soup (No need for the Asian delicacy. Just surround each bowl with florist's grass.)
- Earthworm quiche: Stick some Gummi worms in the quiche.

- Butterfly shrimp
- Garden patch pizzas: Bake refrigerated crescent rolls according to package directions. Cool, then spread with mixture made by combining 8 ounces cream cheese, 1 tablespoon milk, and dash of garlic powder. Arrange rows of vegetables (sliced carrots, broccoli florets, alfalfa sprouts, sliced radishes, and so on) on top.
- Poppy seed muffins
- Cinnamon rolls
- Trail mix

DESSERT IDEAS

- Bird's nest cake: Top a frosted cake with shredded coconut, piling some to make nests. Place egg-shaped candies or jellybeans in nests.
- Cake decorated to look like a birdhouse (Include the message "Turning 30 Is for the Birds!")
- Sugar cookies decorated with bird or birdhouse designs
- Bird's nest cookies: Combine 12 large crushed Shredded Wheat biscuits with 12 ounces melted chocolate chips and ½ cup chunky peanut butter. Use tablespoon to drop mixture onto wax paper. Use the bowl of the spoon to make a nest, then fill nest with jellybeans.

PARTY FAVORS AND PRIZES

- Decorated bag of birdseed
- Decorated tin of trail mix
- Egg-shaped candies wrapped in cellophane and tied with ribbon

GIFT SUGGESTIONS

- Bird watcher's gift basket or backpack: Include binoculars, bird identification guide, journal, and bag of trail mix.
- Coffee-table book about birds
- Ornamental birdcage with thirty one-dollar bills inside
- Decorative birdhouse or garden birdbath
- Live bird and cage (Check with the honoree first!)

Old as Dirt!

Someone's hittin' thirty? That's darn near old as dirt! Rustle up some fun for the old-timer at a western-flavored party.

INVITATIONS

Use invitations with a cowboy or western motif. On the inside write:

[Name]'s
Hittin' Thirty, and That's Darn Near
Old as Dirt!
Ride On Over to the Big "3-0" Corral
and Rustle Up Some Fun
on [Date] at [Time]
[Address]

Or consider these invitation designs:

- Pour some dirt into a plastic sandwich bag and attach it to the invitation.
- Attach a cowboy boot ornament to the invitation.
- Use invitations with an over-the-hill motif. Wrap a bandanna around each.

Whichever invitation design you choose, include a note inviting guests to wear western attire and bring old-as-dirt items like worn-out clothing, outdated accessories, or anything ancient, obsolete, or otherwise worthless for a special ceremony.

DÉCOR

- Hang a banner that reads "Happy 30th Birthday, Old-Timer!" on the wall.
- Cover tables with cowhide-print fabric. For a centerpiece, place a black cowboy boot on top of a pile of sand. Attach a bunch of balloons with an over-the-hill motif to the boot. Or place a bouquet of sunflowers in the boot.

- Use red-and-white-checked or red flannel tablecloths. Arrange cowboy boots, enamel or metal coffeepots, and cowboy hats and use as centerpieces.
- Place small plants in tin or enamel coffee cups or beer mugs. Tie a place card to each handle or attach it to a stick stuck in the plant. Or paint a guest's name on the side of each cup or mug.
- Use bandannas as napkins. Slip each through a rope lasso or around a toy six-shooter.
- Attach tombstones made from poster board to chair backs. Write the name of a legendary western character, such as Billy the Kid, Annie Oakley, or Buffalo Bill, on each. Or hang a toy cowboy hat on each chair back.

THEME-INSPIRED ACTIVITIES

- Have a Big "3-0" Corral shootout: Tack pie tins along the top of a fence or fence prop. Using florist's clay, mount a candle onto each pie tin. Light each candle and give each shooter a squirt gun. Have them take ten paces back from the fence. Instruct shooters to snuff out their candles at your signal. The shooter who snuffs his or her candle out first wins a prize.
- Hold an over-the-hill relay race: Provide a large obstacle for players to climb over. For example, your "hill" could be a stack of tires, a picnic table, the bed of a pickup truck, or a pile of leaf-filled lawn bags. Place a dirt-filled box several yards away from the obstacle. Divide players into two teams and time each team as one by one, its members carry a child's sand pail and shovel over the hill to the dirt, shovel the dirt into the pail, and return to the front of the line. Award prizes to the winning team.
- Have an Old as Dirt ceremony: Bury the old-as-dirt items brought by guests. Give the honoree a shovel tied with black ribbon to dig a hole. Share a few good-bye words and mark the spot with a special tombstone.
- Let guests kick up their heels to some country-western tunes. Hire an instructor to teach guests line dances.
- Project a classic western movie on a wall.

MENU IDEAS

- "Branded" salad: Pour dressing onto a tossed salad in the shape of the honoree's first initial.
- Grilled hamburgers or steaks
- Chili served with grated cheese, sour cream, and salsa
- Corn bread and soda biscuits
- Spicy chicken wings
- Baked beans
- Coffee and bottles of beer

DESSERT IDEAS

- Coffeecake sprinkled with brown sugar
- Dirt cake: Crumble Oreo cookies on top of a sheet cake. Stick in a toy plastic shovel and attach a note that reads "Old as Dirt!"
- Dirt bucket cake: Cut a chocolate cake into 1-inch cubes. Place alternate layers of cake cubes and chocolate pudding in a bucket. Crumble Oreo cookies on top.
- Root beer floats served in beer mugs
- Dirt ice cream: Crumble Oreo cookies into bowls of ice cream. Serve with small plastic toy shovels.

PARTY FAVORS AND PRIZES

- Toy shovel with lemon drops: Place lemon drops in the scoop, wrap with cellophane, and tie with ribbon.
- Bottle of hot sauce
- Dirt (brownie mix) in a red flannel bag
- Package of beef jerky tied with ribbon

GIFT SUGGESTIONS

- Pair of cowboy boots
- Country-western CDs or cassettes buried in a bucket of dirt
- Antiques
- Potted money tree: Attach thirty one-dollar bills to the branches.

An Incredi-Bowl Party

This "incredi-bowl" party is sure to bowl over the honoree!

INVITATIONS

Use invitations with a bowling motif. On the inside write:

You're Invited to
[Name]'s
"Incredi-Bowl" 30th Birthday Celebration
on [Date] at [Time]
[Bowling Alley Name and Address]

Or consider these invitation designs:

- Write party details on a plastic or inflatable bowling pin.
- Have bowling shirts made for the occasion and enclose one in a large envelope.
- Enclose a roster of the birthday bowling team.
- Attach a novelty bowling ball to the invitation.

DÉCOR

Since this party is held at a bowling alley, decorating is super easy. Set up a buffet table behind the lanes and use any of these ideas to decorate:

- Use celebration-motif paper tableware.
- Stick flowers in the finger holes of a bowling ball and use as a centerpiece. Or cut off the tops of thirty plastic toy bowling balls and fill them with flowers.
- Use a bowling pin and ball piñata as a centerpiece.
- Make a centerpiece out of bowling trophies. Set it on a raised platform and surround it with bowls of treats.

- Arrange bottles of beer and soft drinks to look like bowling pins set in V-formation.
- Trim the table with a garland made of bowling towels.

THEME-INSPIRED ACTIVITIES

- Divide the guests into teams. Ask each team to come up with a team name. Award trophies to the teams with the highest score, the score closest to thirty, and the score closest to a random number drawn before the game.
- Rocket Bowl: If possible, hold the party when the bowling alley offers Rocket Bowl (see Party on Planet 16 on page 49).
- Rock 'n' Bowl: Arrange to have the honoree's favorite rock 'n' roll tunes played during the party.
- Blow 'n' Bowl: Cut off the tops of thirty plastic bowling pins. Stick a taper candle in each pin and set them in V-formation. Have the honoree make a wish, blow out the candles, then try to knock them down with a plastic bowling ball.

MENU IDEAS

- Bowling pin pizza: Mold pizza dough into a bowling pin shape or arrange the toppings into a bowling pin design.
- Hot dogs
- Turkey sandwiches
- Chips and salsa
- Beer and soft drinks

DESSERT IDEAS

- Sheet cake decorated with bowling balls and pins and message like "You're Incredi-Bowl!" or "Let the Good Times Roll!"
- Two cakes shaped like bowling pins, with "3" written on one and "0" written on the other
- Sugar cookies decorated with bowling pin or bowling ball designs

PARTY FAVORS AND PRIZES

- Bowl of Whoppers and foil-wrapped chocolate bowling pins (Wrap the bowl in cellophane and tie with ribbon.)

- Bowling alley gift certificate
- Bowling towel

GIFT SUGGESTIONS

- Bowling ball and bag
- Bowling shirt
- Bowling alley gift certificate
- Thirty long-stemmed roses delivered in stages throughout a day (Sure to bowl anyone over!)

Fabulous Fortieth Birthday Parties

Reaching the big 4-0 can be a little scary. Some believe the age officially makes one over-the-hill. Others feel that by forty, all the good times have been had. But here's the truth: Forty is fabulous. Many forty-year-olds discover that life, like wine, is delicious when aged. After a couple of decades of adulthood, forty-year-olds have a better understanding of what they want and how to go about getting it.

So use one of the themes on the following pages to plan a fabulous fortieth birthday party for someone who appreciates the benefits of having lived forty years, who doesn't take turning forty too seriously, or who knows how to kick up his or her heels and cook up some fun.

Classic Winetasting

Celebrate a fortieth birthday with an evening spent cherishing classic art and literature, eating scrumptious hors d'oeuvres, and tasting fine wines.

INVITATIONS

Use invitation note cards with a winery or wine bottle motif. On the front write:

Classics Are to Be Cherished...
Dickens' Literature,
Museum Masterpieces,
Fine Wine, and...

On the inside write:

...Fortieth Birthdays!
Come Celebrate
[Name]'s Fortieth Birthday
at a Classic Winetasting
[Date], [Time]
[Address]

Or consider these invitation designs:

- Glue the invitation on the inside cover of an inexpensive literary classic.
- Attach the invitation to a miniature painting (available at craft or art supply stores) or a framed art postcard.
- Write party details between the staffs on blank sheet-music paper. Add music notes. Roll the invitation into a scroll along with a sheet of classical music. Tie the scroll with black ribbon.
- Copy a photo of the honoree. Cut out the face and glue it over the face on a copy of a famous painting, such as Leonardo da Vinci's *Mona Lisa*. Cut out the painting and glue a Popsicle stick at the base. Tie with ribbon imprinted with the words "Art on a Stick." (Order ribbon from your local stationer or a mail-order stationery company.)

DÉCOR

- Paint the words "Classics Are to Be Cherished! Happy Birthday, [Name]!" on a canvas. Frame it with decorated gold poster board and display it on an easel at the entrance.
- Hang prints or posters of famous works of art on the walls. For fun, make copies of a photo of the birthday honoree, cut out his or her face, and tape the cutouts over the subjects' faces.
- Play classical music in the background.
- Set up several small tables on which to serve the wines. Stock each table with several small plastic cups and a bucket. Use canvas drop cloths splattered with several different colors of paint as tablecloths.
- Design centerpieces inspired by famous works of art or literature. For example, place a bouquet of sunflowers in a vase to represent Vincent van Gogh's *Fourteen Sunflowers in a Vase*. Set out crystal bowls with water lilies floating in them to represent Claude Monet's *Water Lilies*. Arrange a table with a white cloth, apples and oranges in white bowls, and a flowered pitcher to represent Paul Cézanne's *Apples and Oranges*. (Visit www.artchive.com to view these and other famous works of art.)
- Write the name of each wine on a blank sheet-music paper and display it on a music stand next to the table serving the wine.
- Serve hors d'oeuvres on small framed prints of famous works of art.

THEME-INSPIRED ACTIVITIES

- For the winetasting, provide a variety of wines or assign each guest to bring a certain kind of wine to the party. Hire a wine expert (contact a caterer or liquor store for sources) to lead guests in the winetasting. Or consult wine books, magazines, or web sites to learn how to lead a winetasting. Give guests pencils and paper so they can write down their impressions of each wine. Set pitchers of water, glasses, and a dump bucket on each wine table. Have plenty of hors d'oeuvres on hand. (See Menu Ideas.) For fun, pair wines with literary classics. For example, place a copy of *Great Expectations* on the table serving a rich Burgundy or a copy of *The Adventures of Tom Sawyer* on the table serving a sweet Sauternes.

- Play Name That Title and Artist: In the lower left corner, number each print and poster hanging on the walls. (See Décor.) Greet each guest with a program that shows the works of art displayed. (Number each work to match the numbers on the prints or posters.) Have guests write down the titles and artists of the works. Award a prize to the guest who guesses the most correct titles and artists. Collect the programs for a prize drawing.
- Play Pin the Ear on van Gogh: Cut out several right ears from poster board. Tape a large copy of Vincent van Gogh's *Self-Portrait with Bandaged Ear* on the wall. Blindfold each player, spin him or her around, and have him or her pin an ear on van Gogh. Award a prize to the player who pins the ear closest to the correct spot.
- Compose a song for the birthday honoree set to his or her favorite music. (See Supplier Resource Directory.) Include facts from his or her life in the lyrics. Record an instrumental version of the song on cassette. Write the lyrics on sheet music and make copies for the guests. Serenade the birthday honoree with the song and give him or her a framed copy of the sheet music.

MENU IDEAS

- Variety of cheeses
- Caviar on toast points
- Strawberries
- French bread or plain crackers (to cleanse tasters' palates)

DESSERT IDEAS

- Cake decorated to look like the cover of a literary classic (Include the phrase "Classics are to be cherished!")
- Cake decorated with a picture of a classical music composer or sheet music of a classical work (Have a baker re-create the original image. Or if using the real thing, back it with wax paper first and set it on the cake wax side down.)
- Cake decorated to look like a famous work of art
- Assortment of European dessert masterpieces, such as German chocolate cake, French chocolate chestnut torte, English Victoria sponge cake, and Italian *zuppa inglese* (similar to a trifle)

PARTY FAVORS AND PRIZES

- Wineglass engraved with a name of a classical composer
- Miniature bottle of wine
- Classical music CD or cassette
- Print or poster of a famous painting or sculpture

GIFT SUGGESTIONS

- Framed print of a favorite painting
- Tickets to the symphony
- Tickets to an art museum or gallery
- Leather-bound copy of a literary classic
- Collection of classical music on CD or cassette

Cookin' Up a Party

Here's a party that's really cookin'! Partygoers gather in the kitchen and cook up a delicious meal for the honoree. *Bon appétit!*

INVITATIONS

On decorated recipe cards write:

Recipe for Cookin' Up
a 40th Birthday Bash for [Name]

Great friends
Scrumptious food
Infectious laughter
Get-up-and-dance music

Combine all ingredients
for 1 fun evening.
Serve during a Cooking Party
on [Date] at [Time], [Address].

Or consider these invitation designs:

- Write or paint "Cookin' Up Some Fun" on a wooden spoon. Attach it to the invitation with red-and-white-checked ribbon.
- Have party details silk-screened onto a chef's hat or apron. Or write party details on either with a fabric pen.
- Write party details on a poster board cutout of a chef's hat, cook's apron, or wooden spoon.
- Attach the invitation to a set of measuring spoons.
- Glue the invitation over the label on a spice jar or can of food.

Whichever invitation design you choose, include a note inviting each guest to bring an ingredient for a Mystery Stew.

DÉCOR

- Make a sign that reads "Come on in! The party's cookin' in the kitchen!" Draw a chef on it and tape balloons to it. Post the sign on the front door or attach it to a life-size chef or butler cutout.
- Tape balloons with a fortieth birthday motif to the walls or float them to the ceiling.
- Use red-and-white-checked tablecloths. Using a fabric pen, write guests' names on chef's hats and set one on each plate. Lay an apron over each chair back. Tie after-dinner mints, wrapped in red-and-white-checked gingham, to wooden spoon favors. For centerpieces, arrange several bottles of wine or fill baskets with French bread and fruit. Or set flower bouquets in empty food cans (don't remove labels) or in cans that have uncooked spaghetti noodles glued vertically around the outside and are tied with red-and-white-checked ribbon.
- Coordinate table decorations to match the cuisine. For example, use piñatas and a bright green, red, and white color scheme for a Mexican menu. Play mambo and tango tunes and serve margaritas. Or for a gourmet menu, use a black-and-white color scheme. Place Gerbera daisy blooms in martini glasses and set one at each place setting. Play snappy lounge music and serve cocktails.

THEME-INSPIRED ACTIVITIES

Cooking up a fantastic meal is the goal of this party. Plan the menu before the party and buy all necessary ingredients. Or assign guests to bring the ingredients. Some menu ideas include:

- Honoree's favorite menu
- Italian feast
- Chinese meal
- Indian dishes
- Chili or appetizer cook-off: Divide guests into teams and have them compete to make the tastiest chili or appetizers.

In addition to the cooking, entertain guests with these kitchen capers:

- Hold a recipe treasure hunt: Before the party, hide the nonperishable ingredients around the party area. Divide the players into teams and give each team a recipe card listing the hidden ingredients.

Give each team a grocery sack and have them hunt for the items for five minutes. Award prizes to the team that finds the most ingredients.

- Hold a lemon relay: Tape two long strips of crepe paper side by side to the floor. Divide the players into two teams. Have half of each team gather at one end of each strip and have the other halves gather at the other ends. At your signal, a player from each team uses a pencil to push a lemon down the strip as fast as possible without letting the lemon roll off. If the lemon rolls off, the player must start again at the beginning. When the player reaches the end, his or her teammate pushes the lemon down the strip in the opposite direction. Award prizes to the team that finishes first and assign KP (kitchen police) duties to the losing team.
- Make a Mystery Stew: Have guests toss the ingredients they brought into a stew pot. Add broth or water, if necessary. Mix the ingredients together and simmer. Let the guests dig in—or dare them to taste it! It's a mystery if this stew will be edible!

MENU IDEAS

To tide guests over as they cook up the menu, provide chips and salsa or an antipasto platter plus ice water, coffee, or wine.

DESSERT IDEAS

- Baked Alaska
- Strawberry cheesecake
- Grand Marnier soufflé
- Cake decorated with a chef and the words "Cookin' Up Forty"
- Cake baked and decorated at the party

PARTY FAVORS AND PRIZES

- Leftovers in a sealed container wrapped with ribbon
- Inexpensive cookbook
- Kitchen gadget, such as a melon baller, garlic press, or pie vent
- Box of chocolate after-dinner mints

GIFT SUGGESTIONS

- Bread machine, food processor, cappuccino machine, or other modern kitchen appliance
- Forty one-dollar bills in a ceramic mixing bowl
- Ethnic cookbook with matching CD or cassette
- Bottle of wine with a decorative cork
- Gourmet cooking classes

Holy Cow! Look Who's Forty!

Turning forty is no reason to have a cow! Instead, it's a great reason to celebrate with a "moo-velous" birthday party.

INVITATIONS

Use invitations with a cow motif. On the inside write:

Holy Cow! Look Who's Forty!
You're Invited to
a "Moo-velous" Birthday Party
for
[Name]
[Date] at [Time]
[Address]

Don't "Udder" a Word! It's a Surprise!

Or consider these invitation designs:

- Glue the invitation onto an empty milk carton.
- Wrap the invitation in cowhide-print fabric. Tie with coordinating ribbon.
- Attach the invitation to a small toy cow. Add a pipe-cleaner halo to make the cow "holy."
- Cut out a picture of a cow and glue it onto a note card. Copy a photo of the honoree and cut out the face. Glue the cutout over the cow's face. Write party details inside.
- Glue the invitation onto a box of Milk Duds.

DÉCOR

- On a large sheet of newsprint, draw cows grazing in pastures. Tape the mural to the wall.
- Set up a life-size cow cutouts or props around the room. Add halos made of wire and gold tinsel garland.
- Hang black-and-white streamers from the ceiling. Accent with black and white balloons.
- Cover tables with cowhide-print fabric. Or use green tablecloths. Use cowhide-print paper plates and cups. Use plush cows or wood cows as centerpieces. Accent them with pipe-cleaner halos.
- Take inspiration from Gelett Burgess's poem "The Purple Cow" and decorate with a purple cow motif. Use purple linens and use cows cut out from purple poster board as centerpieces. Glue a copy of Burgess's poem onto single-serving milk cartons and set one at each place setting.
- Attach angel wing and halo costume accessories to each chair back.

THEME-INSPIRED ACTIVITIES

- Hold a milking relay race: Set up milking stools next to the cow props or cardboard cutouts. Make cow udders by filling disposable gloves with milk. Prick holes into the tips of each finger. Set galvanized pails under the udders and have players race to milk the most within an allotted time. Award a prize to the winner.
- Cut off the head of a cow cardboard cutout. Take instant snapshots of guests putting their heads above the cow's neck. Write "You Look Moo-velous!" on the snapshots and give as favors.
- Hold a cud-chewing contest: Have players compete to chew the largest wad of bubble gum. Keep track of the number of bubble gum pieces players chew. Award a prize to the winner.
- Play Clothespin Drop: Have players try to drop as many clothespins as they can from nose level into a milk bottle. Award a prize to the winner.
- Clear a dance floor and have guests dance to country-western tunes. Hire an instructor to teach guests line dances.
- Toast the honoree with milk or champagne poured into small milk bottles (available at craft supply stores).

MENU IDEAS

- Cheese-and-cracker tray
- Tossed green salad
- Steak and mashed potatoes
- Steamed vegetables
- Small bread loaves, served with hand-churned butter
- Coffee

DESSERT IDEAS

- Cake decorated with a cow design
- Variety of fruit and cream pies
- Purple Cow cookies and ice cream: Serve sugar cookies decorated with a purple cow design and purple ice cream.
- Black cows (root beer floats)

PARTY FAVORS AND PRIZES

- Candy in cowhide-print bags (cloth or paper) tied with black ribbon
- Box of Milk Duds
- Small wooden cow
- Small milk bottle filled with black and white jellybeans
- Cow-design T-shirt

GIFT SUGGESTIONS

Ask guests to pitch in for one of these group gifts:

- Bed-and-breakfast weekend
- Antique made of milk glass
- Jewelry in a small velvet box placed in a box of milk chocolates
- Telescope to view the Milky Way

Fantástico Birthday Fiesta

Celebrate this milestone with a Mexican fiesta. Dance the fandango, break a piñata, and have a strolling mariachi band serenade the birthday *señor* or *señorita*.

INVITATIONS

Use invitations with a Mexican motif. On the inside write:

¡Ay Caramba!
[Name]'s Turning Forty!
Come for Some
Fantástico Fun at a
Birthday Fiesta
on [Date] at [Time]
Casa de [Host's Last Name]
[Address]

Or consider these invitation designs:

- Attach the invitation to a plastic chili pepper. Or use invitations with a chili pepper motif. Enclose chili-pepper-designed confetti.
- Glue the invitation over the label on a bottle of hot sauce.
- Write party details on a flour tortilla with a marker. Or if you have a telephone answering system that has mailboxes, use a mailbox to record the invitation with mariachi music playing in the background. Write your telephone number on the tortilla, mail it in a plastic sandwich bag, and instruct guests to call the number.
- Paint the invitation on (or attach it to) a sombrero.

DÉCOR

Hold the party on a patio. Or create a patio indoors.

- Light the entrance and outline the area with luminarias.
- Set pepper trees and cacti in clay pots around the room. Decorate with chili pepper lights.
- Set colorful flowering plants in burro-and-cart planters.
- Hang a piñata shaped like a donkey or the numeral "40" from the ceiling.
- String twinkle lights across the ceiling. Drape brightly colored streamers and garlands on the walls.
- Write each guest's name on a balloon designed like a chili pepper. Tie the balloons to a pole.
- Use brightly colored tablecloths. Arrange maracas and paper flowers around sombreros or small cacti in clay pots and use as centerpieces.
- Throw colorful serapes over several chair backs.
- Tie napkins with raffia decorated with plastic chili peppers.
- Line clay flowerpot saucers with brightly colored paper plates.
- Pour water over towels set in a heated clay saucer. Offer towels to guests after the meal.

THEME-INSPIRED ACTIVITIES

- Hire a mariachi band to serenade the honoree and entertain guests.
- Hire dancers to perform a fandango number. If possible, have them instruct guests how to dance the fandango.
- Clear a dance floor and hire a deejay to play a variety of Latin-American tunes. Guests can mambo, salsa, and tango.
- Break the piñata: Have blindfolded guests try to break open a piñata with a decorated stick.
- Give guests paper cups filled with colorful confetti. At your signal, have everyone toss the confetti in the air and sing "Happy Birthday" in both Spanish and English.
- Play Musical Sombreros: When the mariachi music stops, lay a sombrero on a chair instead of removing a chair.

- Give each guest a salt-rimmed tequila shot and sangria chaser. Or give each a chocolate cup filled with Kahlúa. Toast the honoree before tossing back the drinks.

MENU IDEAS

- Beef or chicken fajitas
- Taco and burrito bar: Offer seasoned ground beef, steak or chicken strips, shredded lettuce, sour cream, *pico de gallo* (relish made of finely chopped jicama, orange, onion, bell pepper, jalapeño, cucumber, and seasoning), guacamole, tortilla chips, Spanish rice, and refried pinto beans or black beans.
- Tamales and *chiles rellenos* (mild green peppers stuffed with cheese and fried with a coating of egg batter)
- Blue-corn enchiladas, frijoles, and *posole* (thick soup made of pork or chicken meat and broth, hominy, garlic, onion, dried chiles, and cilantro)
- Mexican beer, Mexican hot chocolate, and margaritas in a variety of flavors

DESSERT IDEAS

- *Marquesote* (sweet bread or torte made with wheat, rice, or corn flour and eggs) topped with apricots and apricot jam
- Mexican-chocolate cake
- Mexican wedding cakes
- *Sopapillas* (puffy fried bread squares served with honey) and ice cream
- Tortilla chips dipped in chocolate and caramel
- Strawberry margarita sorbets
- Fried ice cream

PARTY FAVORS AND PRIZES

- Bottle of hot sauce or jar of homemade salsa tied with ribbon
- Piece of Mexican pottery
- Small cactus in a clay pot
- Mexican jumping beans
- Large paper flower

GIFT SUGGESTIONS

- Silver and turquoise jewelry
- Striped serape
- Vacation at a Mexican beach resort
- CD or cassettes of south-of-the-border music placed in a sombrero
- Mexican cookbook
- Gift certificate to a Mexican restaurant

Nifty Fiftieth Birthday Parties

Isn't it nifty? Someone's turning fifty! Well, some people may need some convincing before they're able to welcome this milestone. The worries are endless: Face-lift or no face-lift? Is the succulent taste of onion rings worth the indigestion? Does gray hair really look distinguished? Is it time to take up knitting and buy a rocking chair?

The honoree may need some time to sort through this nonsense before realizing that turning fifty needn't mean a mind-and-body breakdown. So help him or her see things straight. Throw a birthday party that celebrates a great sport, a cool decade, a stellar career, or a wild streak!

Hole-in-One Celebration

You're sure to sink a hole in one with this fiftieth birthday party. Golf, good food, and great friends—what more could a birthday golfer want?

INVITATIONS

Use invitations with a golf motif. On the inside write:

You're Invited
to a
Hole-in-One 50th Birthday Celebration
Honoring
[Name]
Party Tee Time: [Date] at [Time]
[Address]

Or consider these invitation designs:

- Enclose a few golf tees.
- Glue the invitation onto the cover of *Golf Illustrated*.
- Place the invitation inside a golf ball box along with a golf ball.
- Write party details on a golf visor.
- Attach a birdie (a toy or origami bird) to the invitation.

Whichever invitation design you choose, if your guests will be hitting the fairway, include a note reminding them to bring their golf clubs and golf attire.

DÉCOR

- Park a golf cart near the entrance. Decorate it with a sign that reads "Happy Hole-in-One Birthday, [Name]!" and a bunch of balloons with a fiftieth birthday motif.
- Use green tablecloths. Or use sections of green felt or AstroTurf to cover tables.
- Set a hole-in-one cup and flag (available at sporting goods stores) on each table. Or for some *Caddyshack* fun, set a plush gopher and small cardboard tubes decorated to look like dynamite on each table.

- Make golf ball topiary trees (see page 14; replace the buttons with golf balls) and use as centerpieces. Or make a golf shoe centerpiece: Slip two tumblers, rim-side up, into a pair of socks. Set them into a pair of golf shoes. Place the shoes on the table. Set flower bouquets in the tumblers.
- Use golf towels as napkins.
- Use scorecards as place cards.

THEME-INSPIRED ACTIVITIES

Playing golf is, of course, the party activity for this celebration. Reserve a block of tee times at a golf course. Or check out reserving a miniature golf course especially for the party. Or choose among these golfing activities:

- Design a miniature golf course in your yard or in a room, complete with water hazards, traps, and tunnels. For added fun, play moonlight golf: Turn out the lights (or wait until dark, if playing outdoors). Prop up flashlights to illuminate the holes. String lights in trees along the greens. Paint golf balls with glow-in-the-dark paint and have players wear glow-in-the-dark accessories (available at novelty stores).
- Set up a driving range, chip-shot practice area, and putting greens in your yard. Hire a golf pro to help players with their drives, shots, and putts. Rent golf video games and a virtual driving range game.
- Have a frozen golf tournament: If you live in an area that has cold winters, hold the party at an ice rink or in a snow-covered park or yard. Design a nine-hole course, using pet food dishes as holes and attaching a flag to each dish. Give each golfer a putter, an iron, and a can of tennis balls. Frozen-golf rules apply: Improve your lie twelve inches on any shot and hole out when you putt to within sixteen inches of the flag.

MENU IDEAS

- Fairway box lunches: Place club sandwiches, potato chips, foursome fruit salad (apple, grape, and orange pieces mixed with whipped cream), and golf ball truffles in cardboard lunchboxes.
- Bagel pizzas
- Tossed green salad
- Chips and dip

- Birdies (hot chicken wings)
- Iced tea and hole-in-one sodas (bottles or cans of soda served with straws decorated with glued-on paper flags)

DESSERT IDEAS

- Hole-in-one cake: At one end of a sheet cake, dig a hole the depth and width of a small paper cup. Plant a novelty flag next to it. Insert cup and cover cake with green frosting. Place a golf ball truffle on a tee at the other end of the cake.
- Golf course cake: Decorate a sheet cake to look like a fairway and add birthday candles hot-glued to tops of golf tees.
- Cupcakes topped with golf ball truffles

PARTY FAVORS AND PRIZES

- Teacup filled with golf tees
- Decorated bag filled with golf ball truffles or a mini trophy cup filled with candy
- Snapshot of guests in a frame decorated with glued-on golf tees
- Gopher beanbag toy
- *Caddyshack* videocassette or DVD disc

GIFT SUGGESTIONS

- Set of golf clubs
- Golf shirt or sweater
- Gift certificate for golf lessons with a pro golfer
- Pair of golf shoes
- Fifty-dollar bill taped inside the lid of a box of golf balls

1950s Sock Hop

Celebrate the honoree turning fifty by taking him or her back to the 1950s. Host a sock hop filled with classic fifties tunes, soda fountain treats, and bubble gum fun.

INVITATIONS

Use invitations with a 1950s motif. On the inside write:

[Name]'s Dancin' into
the Nifty Fifties!
Come Celebrate at a
"Bop Till You Drop"
Sock Hop
on [Date] at [Time]
[Address]

Or consider these invitation designs:

- Write party details on bobby socks with a fabric pen. Or enclose a pair of bobby socks.
- Write party details on a replacement label and glue it over the label of a 45-rpm record.
- Attach a wrapped piece of bubble gum to the invitation.
- Cut out a skirt from pink cardstock. Glue on bits of black furry material in the shape of a poodle and draw a leash. Write party details on the back.

Whichever invitation design you choose, include a note inviting guests to come dressed in 1950s attire. Or for a really nifty twist, invite everyone to come dressed as Elvis Presley or Marilyn Monroe.

DÉCOR

Hold the party in a high-school gym or a restaurant with a soda fountain. Or create a sock hop site in your home:

- Hang a banner that reads "[Name]'s Big 5-0 Sock Hop" near the entrance. Draw life-size rows of bleachers on newsprint and tape the mural to the wall. Mount a basketball hoop at each end of the room. Or set up a soda fountain. Recruit volunteers to sling the hash (serve the meal). Have them wear pink waitress uniforms, 1950s advertising buttons, and name tags with names like Flo and Gertie written on them. If appropriate, have them wear roller skates.

- Hang 1950s attire (poodle skirts, leather jackets, letter sweaters, and so on) on the walls. Tape 1950s movie posters, album covers, and celebrity photos (James Dean, Sandra Dee, and so on) to the walls.
- Have guests check their coats and shoes at the door. Remember, no street shoes allowed on the gym floor! Offer guests pairs of bobby socks or sweat socks to wear.
- Clear a dance floor and cover it with pink, gray, and black balloons. Hang a mirror ball above the dance floor. Rent a jukebox or a replica and set it near the dance floor. Float pink, gray, and black (or pink, turquoise, and white) balloons with ribbon tails to the ceiling.
- Use bubble-gum-pink tablecloths and use 33⅓-rpm records as place mats. Wrap pairs of sunglasses around pastel-colored napkins. Fill stemware with wrapped bubble gum pieces and add straws. Accent tables with 1950s album covers and 45-rpm records.
- Slip place cards partially into bobby socks. Or attach place cards to Slinky toys.
- Make a saddle shoe centerpiece: Slip a pair of bobby socks over two small jars. Set the jars in a pair of saddle shoes. Set small bouquets of flowers in the jars. Place 45-rpm records around the shoes. Or make a floral ice-cream soda centerpiece: Stuff pink tissue paper into a soda fountain glass. Place a bouquet of white carnations in the glass and insert a small red carnation on top. Add a pair of straws.
- Use vinyl-record serving bowls (See Décor for Baby Buggy Boogie, page 10.)

THEME-INSPIRED ACTIVITIES

- Five-cent seating assignments: Make a record for each table using black poster board. Glue a different-colored label onto each cutout. Display the cutouts on the tables. For each place setting at the table, glue a replacement label onto a 45-rpm record, matching the replacement label color to the cutout label color. Set the records on a table near the entrance. Give each guest a nickel upon arrival and have the guests "buy" their seating assignments.

- Play Match the 1950s Song Title: Write titles of 1950s songs on slips of paper and cut each slip in half. Distribute the halves among the players. Ask them to find the people with the matching halves of their song titles. For added fun, ask each pair to sing its designated song.
- Have a 1950s fashion show: Let guests model the 1950s fashions they were invited to wear and award prizes for the most authentic outfits.
- Bop Till You Drop: Hire a "Wolfman Jack" deejay to wear a werewolf costume and spin golden oldies. Have the deejay conduct a Twist competition and Hula Hoop and bubble-gum-blowing contests. Award prizes to the winners.
- Rent a karaoke machine and have guests perform their renditions of 1950s classics.
- Hire an Elvis impersonator to entertain and mingle with guests.

MENU IDEAS

- Hot dogs and cheeseburgers
- French fries served in plastic restaurant baskets or in paper sleeves
- Nervous Pudding (Jell-O mold)
- Tray of crackers, Velveeta, and Spam (Or make the Spam Ring described below.)

Spam Ring

1 can Spam, chopped
1 medium onion, chopped
½ cup chopped olives
2 8-ounce packages cream cheese, softened
1 tablespoon Worcestershire sauce
1 teaspoon lemon juice

Purée Spam, onion, and olives until very fine. Mix with cream cheese, Worcestershire sauce, and lemon juice. Place in a greased gelatin mold and refrigerate overnight. Serve with crackers.

- Soda fountain beverages, such as:
  - Make It Virtue (cherry cola)
  - Shoot One (cola)
  - Natural (lemon-lime soda)
  - Choc In (chocolate soda)
  - Suds (root beer)
  - Thirty-one (lemonade)

DESSERT IDEAS

- All the Way cake (chocolate cake served with chocolate ice cream)
- Twinkies and Sno Balls, served with birthday candles
- 1950s ice cream treats, such as:
  - Burn One All the Way (chocolate malt)
  - Fifty-five and Let It Swim (root beer float)
  - Houseboat (banana split)
  - Mystery (chocolate and vanilla sundae)
  - Patch (strawberry ice cream)
- Banana split pie: In 2 deep pie tins, layer ingredients in following order: sliced bananas, strawberry ice cream, chocolate ice cream, vanilla ice cream, and more sliced bananas. Freeze 30 minutes. Remove pies from tins. (Place tins in 2 inches warm water until pies loosen. Carefully flip tins over.) Stack pies and swirl chocolate syrup on top. Sprinkle with chopped nuts and maraschino cherries.
- Banana split cake:

Cake

1 8-ounce can crushed pineapple
Water
1 18-ounce package yellow cake mix
1 3-ounce package instant banana pudding mix
3 eggs
¼ cup vegetable oil

Topping

2 cups whipped topping
¼ cup strawberry jam
¼ cup chocolate syrup
¼ cup chopped nuts
8–12 maraschino cherries

Drain pineapple. Pour juice into measuring cup and add enough water to make 1⅓ cup. Combine cake mix, pudding mix, eggs, and oil in bowl. Stir in juice, then add crushed pineapple. Pour mixture into 2 greased and floured 9-inch round cake pans. Bake according to cake mix directions. When cool, top one cake with whipped topping, place other cake on top, and cover sides with whipped topping. Spread strawberry jam and drizzle chocolate syrup on top. Sprinkle with chopped nuts and maraschino cherries.

PARTY FAVORS AND PRIZES

Let guests choose among lunch bags labeled as follows:

- Blue Plate Special (wrapped bubble gum pieces glued onto a blue paper plate)
- Big Bopper Breakfast (box of Milk Duds)
- Chicken-Fried Steak (can of Spam)
- Root Beer Float (bag of root beer barrels)
- Elvis Dessert Special (package of Twinkies)

GIFT SUGGESTIONS

- CD or cassette collection of golden oldies, wrapped with gold paper and ribbons
- Fifty-dollar bill placed in a model of a 1950s car
- Pair of bobby socks (Stuff a gift certificate to a clothing store in a sock. The honoree can use it to choose his or her own "Big 5-0" fashions.)
- Gift certificate to a favorite restaurant taped to a blue paper plate
- Coffee-table book about the 1950s

Party-in-a-Briefcase

Pop open a briefcase and surprise the honoree with an instant fiftieth birthday party at the office. Or invite him or her, friends, and coworkers to an emergency birthday meeting after work in your "home office."

INVITATIONS

On an office memo sheet or on telephone message paper, write:

You're Invited
to a
Fortune "50" Birthday Party
for Our Favorite Nine-to-Fiver,
[Name]
on [Date] at [Time]
[Conference Room Number or Address]

Shh! Keep this insider knowledge a secret!

Or consider these invitation designs:

- Write party details on a brown or gray poster board cutout of a briefcase.
- Write party details on a mock stock certificate.
- Mail the invitation in an envelope marked "confidential." Or mail it using the United States Postal Service's Priority Mail service or a courier service.
- Copy a photo of the honoree. Cut out the honoree and glue the cutout onto the cover of *Fortune 500* or other business magazine. Write party details on paper and glue it below the cutout.

Whichever invitation design you choose, include a note asking each guest to bring a wrapped inexpensive office item, such as box of staples or pens. For added fun, invite guests to come dressed as the honoree or as the cartoon characters Dilbert or Cathy. Or have them wear the ugliest or craziest ties they can find. (Have guests vote for the ugliest or craziest ties.)

DÉCOR

- If you're throwing the party in the office, use orange traffic cones to section off the honoree's cubicle or office. Write "[Cubicle or Office] Police Line: Do Not Cross" over and over on a roll of yellow crepe paper and stretch the banner across the entrance to the honoree's space. Tape garlands made of a courier service's shipping labels to the walls.
- Decorate a conference room at the office or a room in your home with colorful streamers, balloons, and "Happy Birthday!" banners. Hand out noisemakers and party hats. Use festive paper tableware or paper tableware featuring the cartoon character Dilbert. Use an open briefcase filled with balloons, shredded paper, and confetti as a centerpiece. For décor with a stock market or currency motif, tape cutouts of bears and bulls to the walls. Use paper tableware and decorations with a money motif.

- For a party held in your home, hang sings that read "Men's Room" or "Women's Room" on bathroom doors. Post a sign that reads "10¢ a cup" above the coffeemaker and a sign that reads "Any item not labeled with your name will be thrown out on Friday" on the refrigerator door.

THEME-INSPIRED ACTIVITIES

- Ring a bell to "open" the celebration and sing "Happy Birthday" to the honoree. Or hand each guest a kazoo and give the honoree a kazoo birthday tribute. For added fun, set a crown on the honoree's head, making him or her king or queen of the office.
- Play What Stock Am I?: Write the names of companies that have stock shares, such as IBM and Microsoft, on slips of paper. Pin a slip to each player's back. Have players ask one another yes-or-no questions to figure out the stocks on their own backs. After the game, use the slips for a prize drawing.
- Hold a favor exchange: Pass out the wrapped items brought by guests, one to each guest. Ring a bell to open the "stock exchange"

and have guests "sell" and "buy" the items among themselves. After a time, ring the bell again to close the exchange. Guests keep the favors they end up with at closing.

- Hold a Mindless Busywork Relay: Divide players into two teams. At the starting line, a member from each team sits in a rolling office chair. At your signal, a teammate pushes him or her to a table, where he or she must staple together numbered sheets of paper in numerical order. Next, the pair heads to another table, where the seated player stuffs the stapled packet into an envelope, seals it, and addresses it to the honoree. The pair then races back to the starting line and tosses the envelope into an "out" box. The player who was pushing now sits in the chair, and the next teammate pushes him or her through the course. The first team to finish wins prizes.

MENU IDEAS

If the party is at the office, ask guests to bring bag lunches or order takeout from a favorite restaurant. Or have a "stock portfolio potluck" and assign each guest to bring a dish from the following categories: hors d'oeuvres, main dish, side dish, salad, or dessert. Or offer this buffet:

- Blue chips (blue corn tortilla chips) and salsa
- Stock options bar (variety of soups, cheese toppings, croutons, crackers, and breads)
- New York Stock Exchange bagel bar (variety of sandwich meats, cheeses, and spreads)

DESSERT IDEAS

- Cake or cupcakes decorated with Dilbert or Cathy cartoon characters, served from a briefcase
- Doughnuts and pastries
- Cake decorated to look like a paycheck, stock certificate, or office memo
- Ice cream served with PayDay and 100 Grand candy bars

PARTY FAVORS AND PRIZES

- Desk or page-a-day calendar
- *Dilbert* or *Cathy* newspaper comic strip and Silly Putty
- PayDay and 100 Grand candy bars

- Pen or pencil imprinted with "[Name]'s Party-in-a-Briefcase"
- Coffee cup with a photo of the honoree transferred onto it

GIFT SUGGESTIONS

- Briefcase or "brief"case (novelty boxers or briefs in a briefcase)
- Electronic organizer
- Leather desk set
- Stock certificate for a favorite company
- Gift certificate to a favorite lunchtime restaurant
- Coffee-of-the-month subscription and coffee mug

Born to Be Wild

Even the most conservative folks will enjoy cutting loose at this biker birthday party for the wild fifty-year-old.

INVITATIONS

Use officially licensed Harley-Davidson invitations. Or use invitations with a motorcycle motif. On the inside write:

[Name]
Was
Born to Be Wild!
Come Cut Loose with
[Him or Her]
at a
Wild 50th Birthday Celebration
on [Date] at [Time]
[Address]

Or consider these invitation designs:

- Attach the invitation to a bandanna and enclose a copy of the sheet music to "Born to Be Wild." Ask guests to bring both items to the party. (See Theme-Inspired Activities.)
- Glue the invitation onto a road map.
- Attach the invitation to a novelty motorcycle or a Harley Hog (toy pig).
- Fold cardstock in half. On the front, glue a childhood photo of honoree on a tricycle or bicycle. Write party details inside.

Whichever invitation design you choose, include a note asking guests to dress on the wild side.

DÉCOR

Hold the party in a local bar or truck stop restaurant. (Unless your guests are bona fide bikers, stay away from rough biker bars!) Or create a wild party scene in your home:

- Recruit a couple of volunteers dressed as tough bikers to be bouncers.
- Decorate the room with Harley-Davidson balloons.
- Park a Hog (real Harley-Davidson motorcycle or cardboard cutout) by a jukebox.
- Line walls with beer bottles on shelves.
- Hang Harley-Davidson leather jackets, advertising signs, and other memorabilia on walls.
- Mount neon beer signs on walls.
- Cover tables with unfolded road maps. Spread clear plastic tablecloths over maps. Use plush toy hogs as centerpieces. Dress hogs in bandanna headbands and leather jackets.
- Use Harley-Davidson paper tableware.

THEME-INSPIRED ACTIVITIES

- Have a progressive party. For example, have everyone meet at your house for appetizers, then move on to a truck stop restaurant for the main dish, and conclude the party at a local bar for cake and beers. If any guests ride motorcycles, have them lead the caravan.
- Clear a dance floor and let guests dance to rock 'n' roll tunes played on a jukebox, spun by a deejay, or played by a live band.
- Rent motorcycle video games.
- Have guests belt out karaoke rock 'n' roll tunes. For added fun, ask willing guests to sing silly children's songs or country music ballads. Watching tough bikers sing innocent or tender tunes is hilarious!
- Play Hog Toss: Have players try to toss plush toy hogs into a motorcycle tire set at one end of a table or bar. Players receive a point for each hog thrown into a tire within an allotted time. Or write point values on empty beer cans, line them up on a table or bar, and have players try to knock over cans by throwing the hogs. The player with the most points wins a prize.
- Have guests tie their bandannas around their foreheads, take out the sheet music they brought, and surprise the honoree with a "Born to Be Wild" tribute.

MENU IDEAS

- "Hot as hell" chicken wings
- Barbecued pork ribs, meat loaf, or chicken-fried steak
- French fries and mashed potatoes smothered with gravy
- Corn on the cob and black-eyed peas with ham hocks
- Corn bread served with honey butter
- Coffee

DESSERT IDEAS

- Variety of homemade pies
- Devil's food cake decorated with a hog-on-a-Harley design
- Harley Hog ice-cream treats: Scoop strawberry ice cream into cupcake liners or small dessert bowls. Add marshmallow snouts, chocolate chip eyes, and chocolate ears (Cut white chocolate into triangles and dye them pink using red food coloring.)

PARTY FAVORS AND PRIZES

- Harley-Davidson T-shirt, key chain, or other memorabilia
- Harley Hog (plastic or beanbag pig on a toy motorcycle)
- Temporary tattoo (Give each "customer" a shot of tequila before applying the tattoo.)

GIFT SUGGESTIONS

- Gift certificate to a Harley-Davidson store or catalog (See Supplier Resources for contact information.)
- Collection of motorcycle movies on videocassette or DVD, such as *Easy Rider,* placed in a motorcycle saddlebag
- Leather jacket and motorcycle cap
- Born to Be Wild gag gifts, such as animal-print lingerie stuffed in empty baby bottles or leather clothing or accessories hung on hangers adorned with baby photos of the honoree
- Biker Tyke tribute: Have a local newspaper print a childhood photo of the honoree on a tricycle or bicycle along with a caption that reads "If you think this biker is nifty, call and wish [him or her] a happy fifty!" The honoree will have fun hearing from well-wishers who recognize his or her photo.

Spectacular Sixtieth Birthday Celebrations

Turning sixty doesn't mean the same thing that it did a hundred or even twenty years ago. Healthier lifestyles allow today's sexagenarians to live more active lives than their predecessors, lives in which retirement may not yet be considered. It's fitting, then, to throw a lively celebration for this honoree. A glitzy affair, an antiquing expedition, a dinner operetta, or even a sizzling soirée may be the perfect spirited party for your honoree.

Puttin' on the Ritz

Celebrate a sixtieth birthday with elegance, dignity—and laid-back fun! Host a black-tie potluck, a party that's both ritzy and casual.

INVITATIONS

Use formal invitations in a black-and-white motif. On the inside write:

We're "Puttin' on the Ritz"
in Honor of
[Name]'s Sixtieth Birthday
with a
Black-Tie Potluck
on [Date] at [Time]
[Address]

Or consider these invitation designs:

- Tie white or black ribbon around the spine.
- Cut out a top hat from black poster board. Write party details on white paper and glue it onto the back.
- Tape-record someone singing party details to an instrumental version of "Puttin' on the Ritz." Make copies and wrap a black bow tie around each cassette.
- Write party details on parchment. Roll, tie with black or white ribbon, and insert in a plastic champagne flute. Wrap in a small gift box.

Whichever invitation design you choose, include a note asking guests to come dressed in black tie and to bring a potluck dish.

DÉCOR

- Roll a red carpet down the front walk and have a formally dressed doorperson greet guests. Provide valet parking. For a special touch, rent a stretch limousine to fetch the honoree.

- Use one long table or several small tables. Set each with white linen tablecloths, sterling silver candelabra, and fine china, crystal, and silver place settings. Hire a white-gloved wait staff. Or decorate a buffet table with several pairs of men's white dress gloves. Stuff a few pairs with cotton batting. Position them to "hold" serving utensils.
- Arrange for someone to wait upon the honoree throughout the party.
- At each place setting, set a champagne glass with a flower bloom floating in it.
- Use a top hat (silk or cardboard) as a centerpiece. Accent it with a cane and a pair of men's white dress gloves. Or stuff cotton batting into the gloves. Place floral foam in the bottom of the hat. Poke one end of a pipe cleaner into the batting in each glove and the other end into the foam. Cover the foam with shredded colored paper. Position the gloves to hold a "60" Styrofoam cutout, "Happy Birthday!" sign, or a photo of the honoree.
- Use a high-heel shoe as a centerpiece. Accent it with a feather boa, strand of pearls, and pair of long dress gloves.
- Place a top hat (silk or cardboard) on the seat of each male guest's chair and drape a feather boa over each female guest's chair.
- Attach place cards to cigars or long cigarette holders, novelty high heels, or small velvet jewelry boxes.
- Use faux-diamond bracelets as napkin holders.

THEME-INSPIRED ACTIVITIES

- To create a contrast between ritzy and casual, have the men check their ties at the door. Offer the women pairs of comfy slippers to wear instead of their dress shoes.
- Show the movie *Puttin' on the Ritz.*
- Clear a dance floor and cover it with metallic confetti. Dim the lights and play "Puttin' on the Ritz" and other jazz favorites.
- Play Top Hat Musical Chairs: Instead of removing chairs, set top hats on chair seats. Players must sit on hatless chairs when the music stops.
- Pop open bottles of champagne and toast the honoree.

MENU IDEAS

Try your luck and have guests bring whatever they desire to the potluck. Or give them some direction by using one of these menus:

- Posh potluck: Assign each guest to bring a ritzy dish, such as caviar, lobster, filet mignon, Ritz crackers and gourmet cheese, and so on.
- Five-star potluck: Assign each guest to bring a gourmet dish, such as roast duck, Chateaubriand, steak Diane, shrimp scampi, julienne stir-fried vegetables, baked potatoes with port wine cheese, and so on.
- Potluck challenge: Assign each guest to bring a gourmet dish created with one of the following ingredients: Spam, hot dogs, hamburger, Jell-O, Tater Tots, cheese spread, and so on.

DESSERT IDEAS

- Flaming baked Alaska or cherries jubilee
- Fortune cake: Have a baker decorate a multitiered cake with edible fourteen-carat gold foiling.
- Ice cream and bananas flambé
- Crème de menthe ice-cream cocktails: Scoop vanilla ice cream into crystal goblets. Pour crème de menthe over scoops. If desired, put chocolate brownie squares in goblets before adding ice cream.

PARTY FAVORS AND PRIZES

- Crystal champagne flute
- Diamond (rhinestone) key chain
- Cardboard top hat full of liqueur-filled chocolates
- Box of Cracker Jack containing a faux-diamond ring prize

GIFT SUGGESTIONS

- Diamond necklace, earrings, brooch, cuff links, or watch inside a crystal champagne flute
- Faux fur coat
- Rolex watch
- Lunch at a fancy restaurant
- Top hat filled with sixty one-dollar bills

Sizzling Soirée

For the honoree confident with him- or herself on the inside and out, here's a celebration that may fit the bill. Host a sizzling birthday soirée that celebrates the sexagenarian's sensuality.

INVITATIONS

Use invitations with a black-and-red motif. On the inside write:

Look Who's
Sexy Sixty!
Join Us for a
Sizzling Soirée
in Honor of [Name]
on [Date] at [Time]
[Address]

Or consider these invitation designs:

- Attach a black silk stocking to the invitation and enclose some cinnamon candies.
- Plaster red-lipstick kisses all over the invitation and envelope.
- Wrap the invitation inside a lingerie gift box.
- Wrap the invitation in black velvet and tie with red ribbon.

Whichever invitation design you choose, include a note inviting guests to come dressed as famous lovers, such as Rudolph Valentino, Mae West, Mark Antony and Cleopatra, or Romeo and Juliet.

DÉCOR

- Hang a banner that reads "[Name]'s Sizzling Soirée!" Attach black silk stockings to the banner.
- Cover tables with black velvet and use arrangements of red roses as centerpieces. Attach each place card to a stiletto-heel shoe.

- Float sixty red balloons around the room. Use red place settings, napkins, floor-length tablecloths, and so on. For centerpieces, place several candles in red glass holders. Set the holders at different heights and place some on mirrors. Or use red lava lamps.
- Use a black-and-white color scheme with red accents. Lay black-on-white polka-dot toppers over black floor-length tablecloths. Lift up the corners of the tablecloths and pin them to the tabletop to reveal red table skirts. Place black dinner plates on top of red chargers. Set black napkins on top of red ones. Tie black velvet ribbon around each of several long-stemmed white roses. Arrange them in a silver champagne bucket and sprinkle red rose petals around the base.
- Write names of sixty-and-older celebrities, such as Sean Connery, Rita Moreno, Paul Newman, and Tina Turner, on place cards. Let guests choose which sexy stars they'd like to be for the evening.
- Wrap red or black garters around napkins.
- Throw black silk stockings over chair backs.

THEME-INSPIRED ACTIVITIES

- Clear a dance floor and let guests lose their inhibitions to salsa, tango, and mambo tunes as well as music by The Temptations, Smokey Robinson, Frank Sinatra, and other sensual artists.
- On a wall, project a racy black-and-white silent movie, such as *The Sheik* or *Flesh and the Devil*, or a color one, such as *Jezebel*.
- Play Pin the Kisser on [Name]: Cut out several pairs of lips from red poster board. Blindfold players, spin them around, and have them each try to pin the kisser in the right place on an oversize photo of the honoree.
- Play Kiss on a Stick: Cut out several pairs of lips of sixty-and-older celebrities from magazine photos. Enlarge the cutouts and glue them onto Popsicle sticks. Write whose lips are depicted on the back of the cutout. Give one to each guest and have them hold the lips in front of their own kissers. Let them mingle and guess the identities of the lips. If a guest guesses correctly, he or she is entitled to kiss the guest holding the lips.
- Toast the honoree with a kiss—a kir royale kiss (cherry brandy and champagne served in crystal champagne flutes). Have guests raise their glasses and blow a group kiss to the honoree.

MENU IDEAS

- Oysters on the half shell
- Hot peppers filled with cream cheese
- Spicy chicken wings
- Garden salad—served with (Paul) Newman's Own salad dressing, of course
- Steak and mashed potatoes
- Vegetable medley

DESSERT IDEAS

- Buffet of chocolate desserts, such as chocolate mousse, devil's food cake with chocolate frosting, and chocolate éclairs
- Flaming cherries jubilee, baked Alaska, or bananas Foster
- Red velvet cake
- Black Velvet cocktails: Pour equal portions of champagne and stout into tall glasses.

PARTY FAVORS AND PRIZES

- Hershey's Kisses in a crystal champagne flute
- Single red rose
- Box of cinnamon candies
- Black velvet pajama bag

GIFT SUGGESTIONS

- Pair of silk pajamas
- Gift certificate for a glamour photo shoot
- CD or cassette collection of romantic songs, wrapped in black velvet
- Bottle of perfume or after-shave
- Sixty red roses delivered in stages throughout a day
- Gift certificate for a massage or spa treatment

Antiquing Expedition

You'll find all sorts of treasures at this party. Take guests on an antiquing expedition to celebrate the honoree's sixtieth birthday.

INVITATIONS

Use invitations with an antique motif. On the inside write:

Come Join an
Antiquing Expedition
to Celebrate
[Name]'s Sixtieth Birthday
on [Date] at [Time]
[Address]

Or consider these invitation designs:

- Write party details on a handled shopping bag.
- Pin the invitation and a small satin bow to a vintage ladies' glove or hankie or to a silk-flower boutonniere or men's dress glove.
- Copy a photo of the honoree. Below the photo, write "Genuine Antique 60-Year-Old." Write party details on the back.
- Enclose an antique calling card.

DÉCOR

Whether you're serving refreshments at your home or having them served at a restaurant or café located along the antiquing route (arrange with the manager first), decorate the tables using these suggestions:

- Place floral arrangements in shopping bags with folded-down rims. Use as centerpieces.
- Use antique calling cards as place cards. Place each card on a pair of vintage gloves, a lace hankie, or a purse mirror. Or tie place cards to bags of marbles or glass bottles.

- On each plate, set a vintage handbag with a bag of lemon drops and a lace hankie inside. Or fill vintage cigarette cases with mints or sticks of gum and set one at each place setting.
- Place a vintage hat on each chair for guests to wear.

THEME-INSPIRED ACTIVITIES

- Take guests to an antique mall or visit several antique shops. Start in the morning and break for lunch or tea. For added fun, divide guests into teams and give each team five or ten dollars. Challenge the teams to buy the best antique for the money. At lunch or tea or at the end of the party, have teams present their purchases and ask them to vote for the best purchase. Award prizes to the winning team and give the purchases to the honoree.
- During lunch or tea, entertain guests with these activities:
  - Play Musical Hats: Number slips of paper and tape them to the insides of the hats set on the chairs. Number additional slips of paper to match those in the hats and put the slips in a bowl. At game time, have guests pass the hats to their right while you play music on a boom box. When the music stops, guests put on the hats they end up with. Draw a number from the bowl, ask guests to look inside their hats, and award a prize the guest holding the hat with the matching number. Play again, if desired.
  - Play What's in the Bag?: Fill a shopping bag with small items, such as a can opener, marble, and feather. Each player puts his or her hands into the bag and feels the items for a minute. Afterward, he or she writes down as many items as he or she remembers. Award a prize to the player who remembers the most items.

MENU IDEAS

Invite guests to order from the restaurant's menu. Or preorder a selection of foods for guests to choose from. If serving refreshments at your home, consider these menus:

- Quiche, tossed salad, and fruit
- Monte Cristo sandwiches, French fries, and coleslaw

- Country Store casserole (made with chicken, noodles, and canned chicken soup), salad, and muffins

If desired, have guests gather in a park and enjoy these refreshments:

- Box lunches (chicken salad sandwiches, vegetable sticks, and fruit salad in cardboard lunchboxes tied with ribbon) and lemonade, served in Mason jars
- Teatime baskets (tea sandwiches, scones, and petits fours in baskets tied with ribbon) and Thermoses of tea, served in teacups

DESSERT IDEAS

- French silk pie
- Neiman Marcus cookies: Add 1½ teaspoons instant coffee crystals, slightly crushed, to a chocolate chip cookie recipe.
- Layer cake set on an antique cake plate

PARTY FAVORS AND PRIZES

- Serious Antique-Shopper Kit (tote bag containing a bottle of water, hard candy or pack of mints, and a small magnifying glass)
- "Antique" mirror: Glue a vintage photograph onto the glass of a hand mirror.
- Good-luck coins and/or a coupon to an antique store, placed in a vintage coin purse

GIFT SUGGESTIONS

- Addition to an antique collection
- Vintage handbag or wallet filled with sixty one-dollar bills
- Gift certificate to an antique store placed in a vintage hatbox or cigar box
- "Shop Till You Drop" tote bag: Decorate a tote bag and write "shop till you drop" on it with a fabric pen. Place an antique pricing guide or antique collector's guide inside.

An Italian Dinner Operetta

Mamma mia! Someone's turning sixty! Celebrate with an Italian dinner operetta in which guests change dinner partners whenever they hear famous Italian opera songs.

INVITATIONS

Use invitations with an Italian motif. On the inside write:

Mamma Mia!
[She's or He's] Turning Sixty!
You're Invited to a
Birthday Italian Dinner Operetta
in Honor of
[Name]
on [Date] at [Time]
[Address]

Or consider these invitation designs:

- Design the invitation to look like an Italian restaurant menu or opera playbill.
- Tape-record the party details with Italian music or an opera recording playing in the background.
- Enclose a novelty Italian flag or postcard of Italy.
- Attach the invitation to a chef's hat or a wooden mixing spoon.

DÉCOR

- Place ferns, marble statue props, and birdbaths around the party room. For a special touch, add a water fountain or use smaller ones (available at gift boutiques) as centerpieces.
- Play favorite Italian and Italian-American recordings, such as Dean Martin's "Volare" and Connie Francis's "Mama."
- Tape posters of Italian landmarks like the Coliseum to the walls.
- Hire a white-gloved wait staff.

- Layer red, green, and white linens on tables. Tie coordinating napkins in knots. Or decorate tables in one-color schemes. If appropriate, set up tables *al fresco* (outdoors).
- Use red-and-white-checked tablecloths. Place taper candles in wine bottles. Let the candles burn until wax drips down the sides of the bottles and use as centerpieces. Slip napkins through napkin rings decorated with glued-on uncooked pasta shells.

THEME-INSPIRED ACTIVITIES

- Stage an operatic dinner partner exchange: Upon each guest's arrival, give him or her a card designating a different seating assignment for each course served. When guests hear an opera song, they move to their next seating assignments and enjoy the course with new dinner partners. Some Italian restaurants employ opera-singing wait staffs; consider hiring one for the occasion. Or hire a local opera singer or student to perform. If these options aren't possible, play famous opera recordings.
- Encourage table talk: Write different conversation topics on opera programs and place one on each table. For example, suggest guests come up with opera titles to reflect their lives, such as "Neapolitan Journeys" or "*Amore*." Or suggest each guest share a moment in his or her life relating to an opera title.
- Instead of serving a dinner, conduct an Italian-wine winetasting: Before the main course, have the wait staff bring each table samples of several Italian wines and platters of cheese, pears, and crackers.
- Play Name That Opera Tune: During one of the courses, play an opera recording or have the wait staff or opera singer sing an opera song. Have the guests at each table collectively guess the title of the song. The first table to guess the song title correctly wins a point. The table with the most points wins prizes.
- Toast the honoree with flutes of champagne.

MENU IDEAS

- Toasted ravioli served with tomato dipping sauce
- Antipasto platter
- Minestrone
- Tossed salad served with Italian dressing and garnished with black olives, pepperoni, and Italian peppers
- Garlic bread and fresh butter
- Spaghetti *alla bolognese* (with a thick, hearty meat-and-vegetable sauce enhanced with wine and milk or cream)
- Risotto
- Lasagna
- Cannelloni with cheese sauce
- Chicken *cacciatore* (with mushrooms, onions, tomatoes, herbs, and sometimes wine)
- Veal parmesan
- Chianti

DESSERT IDEAS

- *Zuppa inglese* (Italian trifle)
- Liqueur-laden cake served with Italian coffee
- Lemon *granita* (frozen dessert made of lemons, water, and sugar)
- Neapolitan ice cream
- Spumoni
- Whole fruit, *Bel Paese* cheese, and Asti Spumanti or Marsala

PARTY FAVORS AND PRIZES

- Bottle of Italian wine
- Jar of homemade spaghetti sauce
- Biscotti and/or Italian coffee in a gift bag
- Opera recording on CD or cassette

GIFT SUGGESTIONS

- Pair of antique opera glasses
- Season tickets to the opera
- Subscription to a wine-of-the-month club
- Trip to Italy (or a trip to an Italian restaurant)
- Collection of opera recordings on CD or cassette

Sensational Seventieth Birthday Parties

Reaching this milestone can be a time for remembering the old days and sharing cherished memories. Host a celebration that takes the honoree down memory lane. Or surprise him or her with a party-in-a-box. Throw a party that celebrates the honoree's inner and outer beauty. Or plan an affair that lets the honoree try his or her luck. Any of these parties is sure to help make some new memories.

Birthday-Party-in-a-Box

When some folks reach seventy, they may think they've seen it all and nothing can surprise them. Well, this theme makes for a perfect surprise party! Party supplies are packed into a box, ready for a spontaneous seventieth birthday celebration.

INVITATIONS

Use solid-colored invitations. Wrap coordinating ribbon around each. On the inside write:

Help Us Unwrap
a 70th Birthday-Party-in-a-Box
for
[Name]
on [Date] at [Time]
[Address]

Shh! It's a Secret!

Or consider these invitation designs:

- Tie the invitation to a small helium-filled balloon and pack the balloon in a box.
- Write party details on a paper pattern that can be folded into a cube. (See page 194.)
- Invite guests with a phone call or an e-mail.

DÉCOR

Since the idea is to surprise the honoree, you could follow convention and have him or her walk into a darkened room where guests flip on the lights and shout, "Surprise!" But this trick is predictable, so why not surprise the honoree another way? Throw him or her off-track by letting him or her see the undecorated party room just minutes before guests secretly decorate it. The honoree will be surprised to see an impromptu party appear in a room he or she was just in. Or blindfold the honoree and have guests quickly and quietly decorate the room. Make any final touches after the surprise. Or let the honoree watch guests rush into the room and whip up a festive atmosphere.

Whichever way you choose to surprise the honoree, use these suggestions to decorate in minutes:

- Pack a box with decorations and supplies, including tablecloths, paper tableware, utensils, balloons, streamers, hats, noisemakers, and so on. Also pack any needed decorating tools, such as tape, scissors, balloon clips, and so on.
- Use large gift-wrapped boxes as tables. Or line up several boxes for a buffet or cake table. Use jack-in-the-boxes as centerpieces.

THEME-INSPIRED ACTIVITIES

- Once the honoree has been surprised, light the candles and sing "Happy Birthday."
- Play a version of *Let's Make a Deal*: Wrap prizes and gag gifts in boxes. Play the part of a game show host, letting players choose or trade among the boxes.
- Instead of serving a meal, have a box social: Ask guests to each bring a dinner packed in a decorated box. Conduct an auction and have guests bid on the boxes. (Give guests play money beforehand.)
- Hold a gift-box drawing: Number slips of paper and wrap each slip inside a small gift box. Number more slips of paper to match those in the boxes. Put the slips in a bowl. Give a box to each guest and draw a number. The guest with the corresponding number inside his or her box wins a prize.

MENU IDEAS

- Deli tray
- Catered box lunches
- Delivered pizza or Chinese food

- Meals from a box, such as macaroni 'n' cheese, Hamburger Helper, and so on
- Juice boxes and cartons of milk

DESSERT IDEAS

- Cake decorated to look like a gift box
- Cupcakes or pastries in a bakery cake box
- Assortment of ice cream in ½-gallon cartons
- Small square cookies decorated to look like gift boxes

PARTY FAVORS AND PRIZES

- Small box of candy or chocolates
- Box of Cracker Jack or animal crackers
- Box of stationery
- Jigsaw puzzle in a small box

GIFT SUGGESTIONS

- Boom box
- Box seat tickets to the theater, ballet, or symphony
- Jewelry box
- Big box of chocolates
- Box of golf balls

A Trip Down Memory Lane

Take the honoree on a sentimental journey, visiting special locations or conjuring up fond memories from the past seventy years.

INVITATIONS

Use antique-white invitations. On the inside write:

You're Invited
to a
Trip down Memory Lane Honoring
[Name].
This Sentimental Journey
Will Begin Promptly
at [Time] on [Date]
[Address]

Or consider these invitation designs:

- Attach the invitation to a toy rowboat or antique-model toy car.
- Write party details on a poster board cutout of a suitcase.
- Glue a black-and-white photo of the honoree onto a note card. Write party details inside. Or enclose a copy of the photo.
- Enclose a map that outlines the itinerary.

DÉCOR

Whether the party is held in one or many locations, decorate each site with mementos and photos from the honoree's life. For example:

- Hang school pennants and enlarged baby, school, wedding, and family photos on the walls.
- Line a garden path or party room walls with folding screens. On them, hang photos of the honoree taken throughout the years. Place

photos and nostalgic items (such as scrapbooks, trophies, and handmade crafts) on tables.

- Display special outfits (such as the honoree's baptismal gown, prom dress, army uniform, or wedding gown) on mannequins.

THEME-INSPIRED ACTIVITIES

If possible, take the honoree on a real trip down memory lane:

- Load guests into a limousine, bus, car caravan, or even horse-drawn buggies and visit different locations special to the honoree. Have a volunteer be the tour guide and explain the significance of each stop. Include several sites from the honoree's past, including his or her childhood neighborhood, first home, favorite family picnic site, and so on. Sites where milestone events occurred (such as his or her birth, graduation, or wedding) also make wonderful destinations.
- Bring clues to present to the honoree before visiting each site. For example, pull out a copy of his or her high-school yearbook before visiting the school's football field. Or enjoy French bread, Brie, and wine in the little French café where the honoree met his or her first love. If memories weren't made in the town where the party is, don't worry. Take the honoree to locations similar to those where the events occurred, bring lots of photos and mementos, and watch the memories come flooding back to him or her.

If holding the party at a single site, bring the memories to the honoree:

- Play a version of *This Is Your Life:* Surprise the honoree with visits, audio recordings, and videocassettes of family, friends, and others who've been special to him or her over the years.
- Provide scrapbook supplies, mementos, and photos of the honoree taken throughout the years and have guests make a scrapbook of the honoree's life.
- Have a Memory Lane Fashion Show: Have guests model outfits from different eras in the honoree's life. Prepare bits of trivia about his or her life during that that time and read them aloud with each modeling presentation.
- Clear a dance floor, play songs popular at different times in the honoree's life, and let guests dance down memory lane.

MENU IDEAS

Dine at a longtime favorite restaurant. Or create a menu based on special memories in the honoree's life. For example, include a:

- Wedding memory: Offer cocktails and hors d'oeuvres served at his or her wedding reception.
- Family-outing memory: Serve Grandma's fried chicken and mashed potatoes.
- High-school memory: Order pizza from a favorite pizza joint.
- Childhood memory: Serve malts or floats.

DESSERT IDEAS

- Cake decorated to look like one the honoree had as a child
- Ice-cream sundaes
- Chocolate chip cookies

PARTY FAVORS AND PRIZES

- Travel mug
- Disposable camera
- Small photo album
- Travel-size toiletries

GIFT SUGGESTIONS

- Framed photos of family, friends, and special occasions taken throughout the years
- Travel arrangements to bring children, a close relative, or special friend to the celebration
- Suitcase or set of luggage
- Tour vacation

Monte Carlo Night

Roll a lucky "seventy" with this celebration full of the high-stakes excitement of a Monte Carlo casino.

INVITATIONS

Use invitations with a casino or gambling motif. On the inside write:

You're Invited
to a
Monte Carlo Night
for a
Winning 70th Birthday Celebration
in Honor of [Name]
on [Date] at [Time]
[Address]

Or consider these invitation designs:

- Glue a pair of dice onto the invitation or enclose a few poker chips.
- Glue a photo of the honoree over the face on a playing card of the queen or king of hearts. Attach the playing card to the invitation.
- Design the invitation to look like a passport. Mark Monte Carlo as a destination.
- Write party details on a postcard of a French Riviera scene.

DÉCOR

Hold the party in a posh hotel ballroom or create a ballroom in your home:

- Roll a red carpet down the front walk.
- Hang pictures or photos of Monte Carlo, Monaco, and the French Riviera on the walls.
- Cover cocktail tables with white linens. Set small lamps or candle globes on them.
- Have the wait staff wear tuxedos or dealer uniforms.
- Rent craps, roulette, and blackjack gaming tables.

THEME-INSPIRED ACTIVITIES

- Hire an entertainment company to manage the casino games. Make play money in various denominations featuring the honoree's face. Give each guest a packet of money wrapped with gold ribbon. Near the end of the party, conduct an auction in which guests use their "winnings" to bid for prizes. (See Party Favors and Prizes.)
- Clear a dance floor and cover it with metallic confetti. Let guests try their luck on the dance floor.
- Toast the honoree with champagne and good luck wishes.

MENU IDEAS

- Gourmet cheeses and fruit arranged to look like a roulette wheel
- Caviar on toast points
- Smoked salmon
- Beef medallions served on petit rolls with béarnaise sauce
- Mediterranean salad
- Monte Carlo Cocktails: Mix 2 ounces dry gin, ½ ounce white crème de menthe, and lemon juice (¼ of a lemon). Shake well with cracked ice and pour into champagne flute. Add champagne and serve.

DESSERT IDEAS

- Cake decorated with edible fourteen-carat gold foiling
- French pastries
- Petits fours decorated to look like pairs of dice

PARTY FAVORS AND PRIZES

- Variety of prizes, such as a crystal vase or bowl, theater tickets, and gift certificate to a French restaurant, that guests bid on using their "winnings" (See Theme-Inspired Activities.)
- Deck of metallic-gold playing cards imprinted with the words "[Name]'s Monte Carlo Night"

- Lottery ticket in a champagne flute
- Small jar of caviar

GIFT SUGGESTIONS

- Diamond watch
- Trip to Monte Carlo or to a local casino resort
- Gold cuff links or a gold charm bracelet
- Coffee-table book about Monte Carlo or Monaco

You Must've Been a Beautiful Baby

The honoree must've been a beautiful baby…'cause look at him or her now! Throw a party that celebrates how beautiful the honoree is inside and out.

INVITATIONS

Use baby blue or pink invitations. On the front write:

"You Must Have Been a Beautiful Baby…"
[Glue Baby Photo Here]

On the inside write:

You're Invited to
[Name]'s
70-Years-Young
Birthday Party
on [Date] at [Time]
[Address]

Or consider these invitation designs:

- Attach the invitation to a small mirror tied to a note that reads "You must have been a beautiful baby!"
- Record the invitation on a cassette, playing "You Must Have Been a Beautiful Baby" in the background.
- Draw a baby face on poster board. Iron a baby bonnet flat, pressing on the front of the bonnet. Cut out the face and glue it into the bonnet. Attach the invitation to the bonnet.

Whichever invitation design you choose, include a note inviting guests to bring baby photos of themselves.

DÉCOR

- Hang enlarged baby photos of the honoree on the walls.
- Glue a collage of baby photos of the honoree onto a large sheet of poster board. Have the guests sign it upon their arrival. Or use a baby book as a guest book.
- Display the baby photos brought by guests on a bulletin board covered in velvet or on a velvet-skirted table.
- Make templates of a baby bonnet and bottle and use them to cut out shapes from poster board. Glue copies of baby photos of the honoree onto each side of the cutouts. Glue each cutout onto a length of ribbon and hang it from the ceiling.
- Use baby blue or pink tablecloths. Or cover tables with baby blankets.
- Cover tables with newsprint. Set out crayons and let guests draw baby faces.
- Use framed baby photos of the honoree as centerpieces.
- Draw baby faces on baby bottles using puffy paint. Remove the nipples, insert straws, and use as drinking glasses.
- Place small mirrors at place settings. Tie a note that reads "You Must Have Been a Beautiful Baby" to each.

THEME-INSPIRED ACTIVITIES

- Play Baby Photo ID: When each guest arrives, ask for his or her baby photo. Display the photos as described in Décor and number each photo. Give guests paper and pencil and have them guess the identity of each baby. The guest who identifies the most babies wins a prize.
- Play baby face Pictionary: On slips of paper, write baby-related words (such as *formula, diapers*, and *colic*) and put them in a bowl. Set a large sketchpad on an easel. Divide the players into teams. Have a player draw a slip and then draw pictures on the sketchpad to describe the word. The player's teammates must guess what he or she is drawing within an allotted time. The team that guesses correctly the most wins prizes.

- Hold a baby food tasting: Remove the labels from several jars of baby food and number each jar. Give each guest several spoons and pencil and paper. Have guests try to identify the food in each jar and write down their guesses. The guest who identifies the most baby foods wins a prize.
- Play Pin the Pacifier on the Baby: Enlarge a baby photo of the honoree and tape it to the wall. Cut out pacifiers from construction paper. Blindfold players, spin them around, and have them try to pin the pacifier on the baby's mouth.
- Gather guests around the piano, provide them with sheet music, and serenade the honoree with the song "You Must Have Been a Beautiful Baby." Fill baby bottles with champagne and toast him or her.

MENU IDEAS

- Baby face pizzas: Use toppings to make faces on miniature pizzas.
- Peanut-butter-and-jelly sandwich hors d'oeuvres
- Pâté and crackers
- Chips and dip
- Miniature tortilla wraps
- Peanuts, M&M's, and raisins served in baby bottles

DESSERT IDEAS

- Cake with the honoree's baby photo transferred onto it and the message "You sure were a beautiful baby!"
- Sugar cookies decorated to look like baby faces
- Ice-Cream Cone Pie (See recipe below.)

18 sugar cones
2 tablespoons butter or margarine
6 ounces semisweet chocolate chips
1 quart strawberry or blueberry ice cream, slightly softened

Crush 12 cones. Melt butter and half of chocolate chips in saucepan over low heat. Add ¾ of crushed cones. Press mixture into 9-inch pie tin and chill until firm. Fill with ice cream. Sprinkle remainder of crushed cones and chocolate chips on top. Twist 6 remaining cones upside down into top. Cover with plastic wrap and refreeze.

PARTY FAVORS AND PRIZES

- Baby photo of the honoree glued onto a small mirror, yo-yo, or rattle
- Baby Ruth candy bar tied with pink and blue ribbons
- Baby mug shot: Have a baby photo of the honoree transferred onto a coffee mug. Place packets of Sugar Babies inside.

GIFT SUGGESTIONS

- Family tree or photo album featuring baby photos of family members
- Music box shaped like a baby grand
- Gift certificate to a glamour photo shoot
- Framed baby photos of the honoree and his or her significant other

Exceptional Eightieth Birthday Parties

People in their eighties may feel as passionate about life as they did when they were younger. So throw a party that celebrates the honoree's passion. Whether he or she is passionate about books or family or whether the honoree has a passion for crazy humor or youthful antics, the themes on the following pages provide exciting parties for the passionate honoree.

Good Old-Fashioned Reunion

Remember the good ol' days with a party that celebrates family, friends, and old-fashioned country living.

INVITATIONS

Use invitations with a countryside motif. On the inside write:

You're Invited
to a
Good Old-Fashioned Reunion
Celebrating [Name]'s 80th Birthday
on [Date] at [Time]
[Address]

Or consider these invitation designs:

- Fold cardstock in half. Glue on patchwork-design fabric cut to cover the front. Write party details inside.
- Enclose a country cat ornament: Cut out a cat from fabric with a patchwork quilt design. Blanket-stitch the edges and attach a ribbon loop.
- Attach the invitation to a jar of homemade jam.
- Write party details on the side of a miniature milk can (available at craft stores).

DÉCOR

Hold the party at a country churchyard, on a farm, or in a town hall. Or create a country scene indoors:

- Place white picket fence props at the party entrance.
- Turn a wagon into a buffet table: Line the wagon bed with patchwork quilts and wrap the wheels and spokes with colorful ribbons or streamers.

- Cover picnic tables with blue-and-white gingham or patchwork quilts. Add bright yellow napkins tied with raffia. Or use white and blue napkins tied with dandelions.
- Tie vintage kitchen aprons together and use to trim tables.

- Use bouquets of daisies or sunflowers in Mason jars as centerpieces.
- Use jars of homemade jam as place cards, printing guests' names on the labels.
- Store bottled beverages in galvanized steel tubs filled with ice.
- Serve lemonade from pretty pitchers. Use Mason jars as drinking glasses.

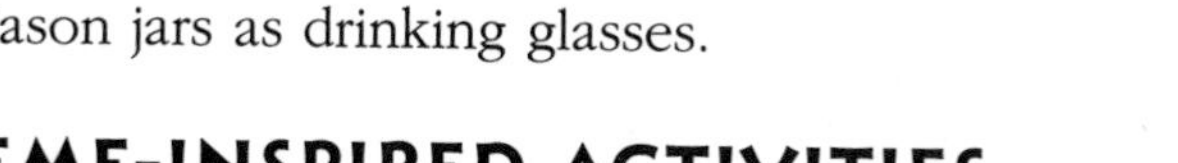

THEME-INSPIRED ACTIVITIES

- Set up horseshoe courts.
- Pile guests into a horse-drawn or tractor-pulled wagon for a hayride. Have a sing-along and bring along cider to wet your whistles.
- Hold a cakewalk: Using chalk, draw a large rectangle on pavement. Divide the rectangle into several smaller rectangles. Number each rectangle. Number slips of paper to match the number of rectangles and put them in a bowl. Play music and have players walk around the rectangle. When the music stops, each player stands in a rectangle. Draw a number. The player who's standing in the rectangle with the matching number wins a cake (or other prize).
- Project a silent black-and-white film on a wall.
- Conduct a pie auction: Provide several homemade pies or ask each guest to bring one. Auction off each pie to the highest bidder. Donate the proceeds to the honoree's favorite charity or use to buy him or her a gift.
- Clear a dance floor and let guests square-dance. Hire a fiddler to provide the music and hire an instructor to teach square dances.

MENU IDEAS

- Roast beef, country ham, or chicken and dumplings
- Corn on the cob
- Fresh vegetables
- Mashed potatoes and gravy
- Homemade bread, fresh-churned butter, and homemade jam
- Bread-and-butter pickles
- Lemonade

DESSERT IDEAS

- Lemonade Pie (See recipe below.)

  1 6-ounce can frozen lemonade
  1 14-ounce can condensed milk
  1 9-ounce container whipped topping
  Graham cracker pie crust

  In bowl, mix lemonade and condensed milk until smooth. Fold in whipped topping. Pour into pie crust. Garnish with sugared lemon slices. (Brush several lemon slices with egg white and sprinkle with granulated sugar.) Refrigerate until serving.

  Variation: Fill bottoms of drinking glasses with mixture of crushed graham crackers and butter. Fill glasses with pie mixture. Add straws or spoons.

- Chocolate layer cake
- Homemade molasses cookies and fresh lemonade
- Homemade ice cream

PARTY FAVORS AND PRIZES

- Jar of homemade jam, pickles, or string beans (Cover lid with gingham.)
- Homemade sugar cookies in a small picnic basket
- Small loaf of homemade bread tied with gingham ribbon
- Vintage hankie

GIFT SUGGESTIONS

- Framed family photo
- Camera
- Antique lemonade serving set
- Rocking chair
- Ice-cream maker

Birthday Bestseller

This bookish celebration is sure to be a runaway bestseller for the birthday bookworm!

INVITATIONS

Use invitations with a book motif. On the inside write:

In Honor of
[Name]'s Eightieth Birthday,
You're Invited
to a
Birthday Bestseller Party
Published by
[His or Her] Closest Family and Friends
on [Date] at [Time]
[Address]

Or consider these invitation designs:

- Glue the invitation into a dust jacket. (Get inexpensive dust jackets at secondhand bookstores.)
- Fold sheets of paper together in half to make pages and write party details on them. Place between cardboard covers. Punch holes along the spine. Thread ribbon through the holes and tie into bows.
- Glue the invitation onto the inside cover of a paperback or hard-cover novel.
- Write party details on paper. Glue it onto a tasseled bookmark.

DÉCOR

Hold the party in a private room of a restaurant, bookstore, or library. Or create a bookish atmosphere in your home:

- Set out several books from the honoree's favorite genre around the room.
- Use a blank journal as a guest book.
- Use black and white tablecloths. Use cloth bookmarks as napkin rings.

- Lay a small book at each place setting. Insert into each a paper bookmark printed with a guest's name. Or write the names of famous authors on place cards and let guests choose their own seats.
- Use a vintage typewriter as a centerpiece. Roll a sheet of paper that reads "It was a dark and stormy night…" around the reel. On each side, stack books and place candlesticks on the stacks.
- Display the cake on a book pedestal or on a stack of books.

THEME-INSPIRED ACTIVITIES

- Choose a book (perhaps one written by the honoree's favorite author) to discuss during the party. Send each guest a copy of the book to read before the party.
- Ask guests to come dressed as characters from famous books. Or ask them to wear items that hint at famous book titles. For example, a guest could wear a small black horse pendant to depict *Black Beauty*.
- Play What Author Am I?: Write the names of famous authors on slips of paper. Pin a slip onto each player's back. Players ask one another yes-or-no questions to figure out the author identities on their own backs.
- Play Book Title Pictionary: Write book titles from different genres on slips of paper. Put them in a bowl and set up a sketchpad on an easel. Divide the players into teams. Have a member from each team draw a slip and then draw pictures that describe the title. His or her team must guess the title within an allotted time. The team that guesses the most titles wins prizes.
- Ask each guest to write a paragraph about a special moment he or she shared with the honoree. Bind these pages together in a decorated scrapbook or three-ring binder for the honoree. Ask each guest to briefly tell the party what he or she has written before toasting the honoree.

MENU IDEAS

- *The **Grapes** of Wrath* **and Cheese**
- *The Secret **Garden*** **Salad**
- ***Chicken Soup** for the Soul*
- ***Fried Green Tomatoes** at the Whistle Stop Café*
- *Real Men Don't Eat **Quiche***
- *The Catcher in the **Rye*** **Bread**
- ***Black Coffee***

DESSERT IDEAS

- Cake decorated to look like an open book
- Cake designed like the cover of the honoree's favorite book
- "Cordially Yours" Ice-Cream Cocktails (See recipe below.)

  8 maraschino cherries with stems
  8 tablespoons brandy
  Powdered sugar
  2 pints chocolate ice cream
  8 jiggers cherry-flavored liqueur

  Marinate cherries in brandy. Dip rims of champagne flutes in water and then in powdered sugar. Freeze glasses at least ½ hour. Scoop ice cream into each glass. Just before serving, pour 1 jigger of liqueur over ice cream. Top with a cherry. Serves 8.

PARTY FAVORS AND PRIZES

- Dime romance or adventure novel
- Bookmark designed with the honoree's photo
- Bag of bookworms (Gummi worms)

GIFT SUGGESTIONS

- Bookcase
- Pair of bookends
- First edition of a favorite book
- Leather-bound literary classic
- Books on cassette or CD

Crazy-80 Dinner Party

This party gives the honoree and eight guests or couples the chance to be crazy at a zany eightieth birthday celebration!

INVITATIONS

Use invitations with a slapstick or joke motif. On the inside write:

"Time flies like an arrow. Fruit flies like a banana."
—Groucho Marx

You're Invited to a
Crazy-80 Dinner Party
to Celebrate [Name]'s
Eightieth Birthday
on [Date] at [Time]
[Address]

Or consider these invitation designs:

- Attach the invitation to a plastic eight ball.
- Glue the invitation onto the inside cover of a joke book.
- Attach a clown nose to the invitation.
- Write party details on a whoopee cushion.

DÉCOR

- Hang streamers and balloons of all colors and shapes from the ceiling.
- Use brightly colored tablecloths with a crazy design.
- Cut out "Crazy 80" from Styrofoam. Throw confetti and streamers over it and use as a centerpiece.
- Adorn the walls with posters of eight famous comedians, such as Buster Keaton, Charlie Chaplin, Lucille Ball, and The Marx Brothers.

- Have the wait staff wear wacky items or crazy articles of clothing, such as oversize sunglasses, colorful suspenders, or stacks of eight hats.
- Stack eight different-colored plates at each place setting.
- For each place setting, individually wrap eight party favors in eight small gift boxes. (See Party Favors and Prizes for favor ideas.) Stack the boxes, write a guest's name on ribbon, and tie the top box with it.

THEME-INSPIRED ACTIVITIES

- Serve a Crazy Eight-Course Dinner in which each guest is served the same eight courses but enjoys the courses in a different order from every other guest. Guests draw playing cards to learn what courses they'll be served. The cards drawn correspond to a numbered menu. To make the dinner move smoothly, make sure all of the courses are ready to serve. And be sure to explain to the wait staff how the dinner works!
    - Display a menu that lists each course. Assign each course a number one through eight. If serving a formal dinner, serve these traditional six courses: soup, fish, main course, salad, dessert, and fruit. Serve appetizers before dinner and coffees and liqueurs after.
    - Place identical hands of nine playing cards at each place setting, each hand containing an ace (number 1), one each of numbers 2 through 7, and two "crazy" number 8s.
    - Have guests hold up their hands of cards (numbers facing toward them) to the guests on the left. Those guests draw a card to find out what course they'll be served. For example, if a guest draws a 3, he or she will be served the third course. If a guest draws a "crazy" 8, he or she can choose whatever course desired, even if it's already been served to him or her.
    - Discard cards after being drawn. Wait until everyone finishes eating their courses before clearing dishes and having guests draw their next cards.

- Play What Comedian Am I?: Write the names of famous comedians on slips of paper. Pin a slip onto each player's back. Have players ask one another yes-or-no questions to figure out the identities on their own backs.
- Rent a pool table and let players knock around the eight ball.
- Give the honoree a musical tribute: Borrow or rent a variety of instruments, such as an accordion, recorder, trumpet, and drum set. Assign guests to play instruments that they've never played before. Allow the orchestra fifteen minutes to practice, and then have them perform their tribute. Or pass out kazoos to all guests and give the honoree a crazy kazoo tribute. What the musicians lack in talent, they'll make up in enthusiasm!

MENU IDEAS

If you choose not to serve the Crazy Eight-Course Dinner as described in Theme-Inspired Activities, serve eight crazy dishes such as these:

1. Velveeta and Spam hors d'oeuvres
2. Build-your-own hero sandwiches
3. Peanut-butter-and-banana (or pickle) sandwiches
4. Fruit salad
5. Jell-O Jigglers
6. Phony bologna: Mold meat loaf into hot dog shapes before cooking. Place in hot dog buns and top with ketchup, mustard, relish, onions, and pickles.
7. Chocolate chili
8. Spam roast

DESSERT IDEAS

- Upside-down pineapple cake
- Make-your-own sundae bar
- Sugar cookies decorated to look like eight balls
- Sno Balls and Twinkies topped with trick birthday candles and served on silver trays

PARTY FAVORS AND PRIZES

Set this stack of crazy-eight favors in gift boxes at each place setting:

- Box 1: Eight Hershey's Kisses
- Box 2: Kazoo
- Box 3: Deck of playing cards
- Box 4: Plastic eight ball key chain
- Box 5: Silly Putty
- Box 6: Joke or limerick book
- Box 7: Note that reads "A can of silly string is underneath your chair. Use it!"
- Box 8: Confetti to shower upon the honoree

GIFT SUGGESTIONS

- Crazy quilt
- Barrel of laughs (Videocassettes of classic comedy movies and TV shows placed in a small wooden barrel)
- Telephone shaped like a shoe, a car, or other crazy item

Young at Heart

You're only as old as you feel. So throw a traditional child's birthday party for the young-at-heart honoree.

INVITATIONS

Use invitations with a children's party motif. On the inside write:

Candles, Cake, and Donkey Tails
for the
Young at Heart!
Come Celebrate
[Name]'s 80th Birthday
on [Date] at [Time]
[Address]

Or consider these invitation designs:

- Place the invitation inside a children's party loot bag.
- Glue the invitation onto a child's party hat.
- Write party details on an inflated balloon and deflate it.
- On a note card, draw a large crayon heart. Glue a childhood photo of the honoree inside the heart and write party details inside the card.

DÉCOR

- Hang colorful balloons and streamers throughout the party room.
- Hang a banner that reads "Young at Heart ♥ [Name] ♥ 80 Years Young" near the entrance.
- Provide paper tableware with a children's birthday-party motif, such as clowns, fire engines, or cartoon characters.
- Pour nuts, butter mints, or gumdrops in paper cups. Set one at each place setting.

THEME-INSPIRED ACTIVITIES

Let both the young and young-at-heart guests enjoy these traditional children's games. If appropriate, have younger and older guests team up, with the younger guests pinch-hitting for the older guests if necessary.

- Play Pin the Tail on the Donkey.
- Play Clothespin Drop: Have players try to drop as many clothespins as they can from the sides of their noses into a bottle. Award a prize to the winner.
- Play musical chairs: Vary the game by having an adults-only round, a kids-only round, and so on.
- Hire a clown to entertain guests with tricks, balloon animals, and face painting.

MENU IDEAS

- Pizza
- Hot dogs, hamburgers, or sloppy joes
- Peanut-butter-and-jelly sandwiches
- Veggies and dip
- Kool-Aid punch: Pour 8 cups Kool-Aid and 2 quarts ginger ale into large punch bowl. Add several scoops of sherbet just before serving.

DESSERT IDEAS

- Cake decorated with a childlike design
- Cupcakes decorated with sprinkles, candy confetti, and so on
- Frosted layer cake decorated with animal crackers, gumdrops, and Lifesavers (to hold candles)
- Ice-cream-cone clowns: Scoop ice cream into cupcake liners. Set sugar cones upside down on top of scoops. Use frosting to draw clown faces on scoops and to decorate cones.

PARTY FAVORS AND PRIZES

- Bottle of bubbles
- Lollipop
- Bag of marbles
- Plastic jewelry
- Pinwheel

GIFT SUGGESTIONS

Fill a red wagon with these gifts:

- Teddy bear
- Carousel music box
- Electric train set
- Remote-control car
- Kite

Creative Ninetieth Birthday Parties

Poet Stanley Kunitz won a National Book Award for his collection of poems, *Passing Through*, at age ninety. Anna Mary Robertson (Grandma Moses) painted *Horse Shoeing* while in her nineties. Antonio Stradivari fashioned two of his most famous violins while in his nineties. And Frank Lloyd Wright designed New York City's Guggenheim Museum at age ninety. These famous figures prove creativity has no age limit. Whether you host a Hollywood gala, a birthday tea, a colorful event, or an ice-cream social, throw a creative party that celebrates the honoree's uniqueness.

Ninety Years in Pictures

Treat guests like Hollywood celebrities at a ninetieth birthday extravaganza starring the honoree.

INVITATIONS

Use formal invitations. On them write or engrave:

You're Invited to
a Hollywood Extravaganza
Honoring
[Name]
to Celebrate [His or Her]
"Ninety Years in Pictures"
on [Date] at [Time]
[Address]

Or consider these invitation designs:

- Place the invitation in a popcorn box filled with tissue paper.
- Tape the invitation to a videocassette box. Stuff packets of microwave popcorn inside.
- Use invitations with a movie or Hollywood motif.
- Design the invitation to look like a movie ticket or script.
- Attach the invitation to a pair of black sunglasses.

DÉCOR

Hold the party in a movie theater. Many theaters rent out their lobbies and auditoriums for special functions. You may also be able to arrange for a private screening of a film. Or create a Hollywood party in your home:

- Hire a limousine to fetch the honoree.
- Write the honoree's name and the words "Ninety Years in Pictures" on a large sheet of poster board. Or cover the poster board with velvet and attach an enlarged photo of the honoree. Display it on an easel.

- Roll a red carpet down the front walk or use chalk to write the honoree's name inside stars drawn on the front walk or driveway. Rent a roving spotlight (or shine stationary ones on the front door).
- Set potted palm trees or silver Christmas trees around the room. Hang framed photos of the honoree from the branches.
- Hang photos of the honoree taken throughout the years around the room. Enlarge a few photos to movie poster size and add film titles, such as *Father of the Bride* or *It's a Wonderful Life.*
- Cover tables with floor-length silver lamé cloths. Use black chair covers and silver lamé sashes.
- Place disposable cameras on tables.
- At the head table, set a director's chair imprinted with the honoree's name inside a star.

- Cut out large stars from poster board and cover them with aluminum foil. Write each guest's name with a gold or silver glitter pen on a poster board rectangle and attach it to a star. Attach the stars to chair backs. For added fun, use the names of film stars and let guests choose their own seating assignments.
- For a centerpiece, arrange a framed photo of the honoree, movie clapboard, and Oscar statuette. Toss silver tinsel over the arrangement and place votive candles around it. On the movie clapboard, write "Ninety Years in Pictures."

THEME-INSPIRED ACTIVITIES

- As guests walk up the red carpet, have the "paparazzi" shoot photos of them. Also, have a "camera crew" on hand to record candid moments of the party and of the guests sending best wishes to the honoree. Show the video on a big-screen TV at the end of the party. Present the honoree with the edited videocassette at a later date.
- Greet guests with autograph books. Have them collect "celebrity" guest signatures. Award a prize to the guest who collects the most autographs. Collect the books for a prize drawing.
- Play Name That Famous Movie Phrase: On slips of paper, write familiar phrases from famous movies, such as "Play it again, Sam" (*Casablanca*) or "Show me the money!" (*Jerry Maguire*). Divide the players into two teams. One team member draws a slip and reads

the phrase to his or her team, which must give the corresponding movie title within an allotted time. If the team can't give the correct movie title, the other team has a chance to guess. Award a point for each correct answer. The team with the most points wins prizes.

- Show a "Ninety Years in Pictures" movie made from edited home movies of the honoree. Or show slides or a video of still frames made from photos of the honoree taken throughout the years. For a special touch, set the show to music.
- Show the honoree's favorite movie on a big-screen TV.

MENU IDEAS

- Popcorn, candy, and sodas
- Buffet featuring dishes from the settings of famous movies, such as Thai food (*The King and I*), French pastries (*Sabrina*), seafood (*Treasure Island*), western barbecue (*City Slickers*), and chocolate desserts (*Forrest Gump*)
- Hollywood cocktails, such as Charlie Chaplin champagne, "Make my day" margaritas, and "Frankly, my dear, I don't give a damn" daiquiris

DESSERT IDEAS

- The Graumann's Chinese Theatre Walk of Fame cake: Have the honoree press his or her (clean) hands into the center of a frosted sheet cake. Have the honoree write his or her name below the hands.
- Cake with a photo of the honoree transferred onto it (Place sparklers around the photo. See Supplier Resource Directory.)
- Frosted cupcakes arranged in the shapes of the numerals 9 and 0
- Marquee cake: Lay twinkling lights around a cake decorated to look like a movie marquee.

PARTY FAVORS AND PRIZES

- Photo of the honoree framed with cardboard star cutout
- Gourmet popcorn in a popcorn box
- Star-shaped tree ornament
- Gift certificate to a movie theater

GIFT SUGGESTIONS

- Bouquet of roses
- Scrapbook filled with photos, mementos, and special notes from the past ninety years
- Television, DVD player or VCR, or video camera
- Videocassettes or DVDs of classic Hollywood movies in a gift basket

Birthday Tea

Celebrate a ninetieth birthday with some of life's simple pleasures: a hot cup of tea, delectable sweets, and warm conversations with friends and family.

INVITATIONS

Use invitations with a teacup or teapot motif. On the inside write:

You're Cordially Invited
to a Birthday Tea
in Honor of
[Name]'s Ninetieth Birthday
on [Date] at [Time]
[Address]

Or consider these invitation designs:

- Attach the invitation to a tea bag or to a vintage hankie.
- Attach the invitation to a teacup and saucer set.
- Enclose a copy of a Victorian poem.
- For a gentleman's tea, use invitations with an English-hunt motif. Or attach the invitation to a tin of English toffee.

Whichever invitation design you choose, invite guests to wear teatime hats and gloves.

DÉCOR

Hold the party at a tearoom in a hotel, department store, or bed-and-breakfast. Or create a tearoom in your home or garden.

- Place a tea service on a buffet table. Or set one on each table. Choose a tea service that fits the honoree's taste. Floral-pattern, sterling silver, or copper (perfect for a gentleman's tea) are popular choices. Add coordinating napkins, napkin rings, tea strainers, and teaspoons.

- Use antique lace tablecloths. Or cover tables with layers of cloths in lovely colors and patterns.
- Hire a string quartet or harpist to play classical music. Or play CDs or cassettes of favorite classical recordings.
- If serving outdoors, place beverage bonnets (crocheted or lace-trimmed cloth circles weighted with beads around the edges) on the tops of drinking glasses.
- Display teacakes and cookies on serving plates, cake pedestals, and tiered serving trays.
- Use place cards with a Victorian motif. Or greet each guest with a place card that has a picture of a flower and its meaning on it. For example, carnation means "love," gardenia means "joy," and lily of the valley means "happiness." Guests sit at the tables that have the flowers pictured on their cards.

THEME-INSPIRED ACTIVITIES

- Play old-fashioned parlor games, such as checkers or charades.
- Play Teakettle: Choose a player to leave the room. The others choose two words that are homophones, such as *so* and *sew*. When the player returns, the others talk to him or her using the word *teakettle* instead of the chosen word. For example, they might say "She's teakettle (so) pretty!" or "Please teakettle (sew) this sock." The player then guesses what word *teakettle* replaces.
- Read tea leaves: When guests finish drinking their tea, have them strain any remaining liquid from teacups and leave the tea leaves behind. Have them shake up the tea leaves, then flip the teacups onto saucers. The shapes tea leaves form on saucers foretell guests' futures. For example, fruit means fairly fortunate times, a harp denotes romance, and a tree symbolizes luck. Consult a tea leaf fortunetelling book for more interpretations.
- Have someone dressed in a Victorian-era costume recite Victorian poems or read from a Victorian novel.
- Play croquet.

MENU IDEAS

- Ribbon sandwiches or cucumber sandwiches
- Salmon-and-cream-cheese pinwheels

- Scones served with Devonshire cream, jams, and lemon curd
- Fruit garnishes
- Variety of teas
- Claret or lemonade

DESSERT IDEAS

- Petits fours with birthday candles
- Miniature fruit tarts
- Walkers Shortbread
- Victorian charm cake: For each guest, tie a charm to one end of a long length of ribbon. Hide the end with the charm under a layer cake, leaving the rest of the ribbon stretched out. Have each guest choose a ribbon and pull out a charm to learn his or her fortune. For example, a heart signifies love, a book means a studious stranger will come into your life, and so on. (See Supplier Resource Directory to learn where to buy charms.)

PARTY FAVORS AND PRIZES

- Vintage hankie
- Decorative canister or box of tea
- Sweet-smelling sachet
- Decorative teacup

GIFT SUGGESTIONS

- Book of Victorian poems
- China tea service
- Antique lace shawl
- Victorian regard ring with gemstones that spell out a special message (For example, a topaz, an emerald, and an amethyst spell out "tea.")
- Gold watch with chain
- Jeweled hatpin
- Gentleman's walking stick

Color Me a Party

Color the honoree a bright, creative ninetieth birthday party that's sure to make guests of all ages smile.

INVITATIONS

Use invitations with a crayon motif. On the inside write in crayon:

Come Color
[Name] a Happy
Ninetieth Birthday Party
on [Date] at [Time]
[Address]

Or consider these invitation designs:

- Write party details in crayon on a slip of paper. Roll it around a crayon and slip it into a crayon box. (Make sure it's noticeable!) Or glue the invitation onto a crayon box.
- Glue the invitation onto a coloring book or write party details on a coloring-book page.
- Recruit kids to draw crayon pictures on paper. Write party details in crayon on the back of each drawing.

DÉCOR

- Hang colorful streamers and float balloons throughout the party room. Hang large inflatable Crayola crayons from the ceiling.
- On a large sheet of newsprint, draw crayon stick figures of family members along with a house, trees, pets, and flowers. Tape photos of the family members' heads onto the stick figures. Tape the mural to the wall. Or tape crayon portraits of family members to the walls.
- Tape large sheets of newsprint to the walls. Encourage guests to draw birthday wishes and pictures in crayon. (See Theme-Inspired Activities.)
- Cover tables with newsprint. Set boxes of crayons at place settings and encourage guests to color. Or use a different color scheme for each table (one table decorated all in red, another in green, and so

on). Greet each guest with a crayon. Guests sit at the tables that match their crayons' colors.

- Use Crayola paper tableware. Wrap napkins with several colorful, thin ribbons tied to crayons.
- Tie a helium-filled balloon to each chair back. Weight a bunch of balloons with a box of crayons and use as a centerpiece.
- Use crayon sculptures as centerpieces. (See Theme-Inspired Activities.) Or fill baskets or opened gift-wrapped boxes with coloring books and use as centerpieces.
- Use coloring-book pages to trim buffet tables or to make a ceiling garland.

THEME-INSPIRED ACTIVITIES

- Invite guests to draw pictures and birthday messages for the honoree. (See Décor.)
- Have a centerpiece sculpture contest: On each table, place a box of crayons, glue, rubber bands, string, and so on. Recruit players at each table to create a centerpiece. Award prizes to centerpieces that are the tallest, most unusual, funniest, and so on.
- Set crayons and white construction paper at each place setting. Have the guests design birthday cards for the honoree.
- Play What Color Is My Crayon?: Tie a crayon to the middle of a long piece of string. Tie the ends of the string together to make a necklace. Pull a necklace over the player's head so that the crayon rests on his or her back. Have players ask one another yes-or-no questions to figure out the colors of the crayons on their own backs.
- Play Crayon Drop: Have players drop as many crayons as they can from nose level into empty milk bottles. Award a prize to the winner.
- Play Blindfolded Crayon Artist: Set out sheets of paper and crayons. Blindfold players and have them draw certain objects. Award prizes for the drawings that are the most accurate, most artistic, and so on.
- Have each guest choose a crayon whose color represents something about the honoree. Ask him or her to share with everyone what the

color represents. For example, a yellow crayon could represent his or her sunny disposition or a green crayon could represent his or her love of gardening.

MENU IDEAS

Place a coloring book at each place setting and glue this menu inside the cover of each book:

- Tossed green salad
- Orange-glazed chicken
- White rice
- Yellow wax beans
- Blueberry muffins
- Black coffee
- Melted Crayon punch [Add 2 packages Kool-Aid mix to 1 can frozen lemonade and 1 liter of lemon-lime soda.]

DESSERT IDEAS

- Crayon cake: Make a cake in the honoree's favorite color. (Add food coloring to white cake batter.) Gather several crayons the same color as the cake. Stick the crayons in the frosted cake.
- Cake topped with candles and crayons, together totaling ninety
- Cake with birthday wishes written in frosting (Let the last word trail off and place a crayon the same color as the frosting at the end of the trail so it looks as if the crayon was used to write the message.)
- Ice cream served in paper cups decorated with crayon (For added fun, glue crayons to spoon handles.)

PARTY FAVORS AND PRIZES

- Thank-you note attached to a box of crayons or rolled-up coloring book
- Thank-you note with a crayon stick figure of the honoree drawn on it (Glue a photo of the honoree's face over the head of the stick figure.)
- Frame decorated with glued-on crayons (Insert a crayoned thank-you note or a photo of the honoree.)
- Crayon box filled with candy

GIFT SUGGESTIONS

- Gift certificate for an art class or to a restaurant, placed in an empty crayon box
- Scrapbook of family photos and crayoned messages from family and friends
- Colorful shawl or cardigan
- Single crayon attached to a homemade coupon: Make a coupon for the honoree to redeem for a service. For example, attach a green crayon to a coupon for a lawn mowing or a walk in the park.

Ice-Cream Social

Treat the honoree to an ice-cream social where guests have some sweet, old-fashioned fun.

INVITATIONS

Use invitations with an ice-cream motif. On the inside write:

You're Invited to an
Old-Fashioned Ice-Cream Social
in Honor of
[Name]'s Ninetieth Birthday
on [Date] at [Time]
[Address]

Or consider these invitation designs:

- Glue a small inflated balloon into a sugar cone. Write party details on the balloon or on a note card attached to the cone. Or spray-paint a cone in a bright color, fill it with colored tissue paper, and attach the invitation to it. Wrap the cone in cellophane, tie with ribbon, and gift-wrap it in a small box.
- Write party details on a postcard of a late-1800s scene.
- Draw a three-scoop ice-cream cone on a white cardstock postcard. Color each scoop a different color. Write party details on the scoops.

DÉCOR

Hold the party in a park. Or create a park indoors:

- Set park benches under potted trees.
- Rent late-1800s-era costumes and recruit a few volunteers to wear them and greet guests.
- Design a mural depicting a late-1800s scene, such as people strolling though a park or riding tandem bicycles, and tape it to the wall.
- Spread blankets on the floor for a picnic. Or use red-and-white-striped tablecloths on tables.
- Make an ice-cream-soda centerpiece: Stuff pink tissue paper into a soda fountain glass. Set a bouquet of white carnations in the glass and insert a small red carnation on top. Add a straw.

- Place flowers in mustache mugs and use as centerpieces or to decorate place settings.
- Using puffy paint, write guests' names on upside-down sugar cones and use as place cards. Or make parasol-shaped place cards by folding paper doilies in half, writing guests' names on them, and gluing handles made of pipe cleaners onto them.
- Set a bag of marbles or taffy at each place setting.

THEME-INSPIRED ACTIVITIES

- Hire a banjo player or a barbershop quartet dressed in red-and-white-striped vests and skimmers to entertain guests with popular tunes from the turn of the nineteenth century, such as "Bicycle Built for Two." Or rent a player piano.
- Rent several late-1800s costumes for the guests to wear for a black-and-white photo.
- Organize a taffy pull or have guests make ice cream. Or have a cakewalk (see page 145).
- Give barbershop makeovers: Invite "customers" to sit on a chair while someone covers them with barber's aprons and paints handlebar mustaches on their faces with grease paint. For willing customers, have the barber slick their hair with gel, parting it down the center. Have an instant camera ready to snap photos!
- Rent tandem bicycles for guests to ride.
- Provide lawn games for guests to play, such as croquet and horseshoes. Have a potato sack race.

MENU IDEAS

Set the following dishes on a buffet table or pack them in picnic baskets:

- Cold fried chicken
- Potato salad
- Fruit or fruit salad
- Cold baked beans
- Vegetable sticks
- Lemonade

- Barney's Ginger Ale (see recipe below): This recipe has been in my friend Peggy's family for years. Her eighty-eight-year-old dad drinks it all summer long, and he claims he's been "healthy as a horse forever."

Barney's Ginger Ale

1 teaspoon ginger
½ cup vinegar
2 cups sugar
1 gallon water
Juice from 2 lemons

Mix all ingredients together. Stick lemon slices on rims of glasses.

DESSERT IDEAS

- Ice-cream cake: Make your own by spreading ice cream between layers of cake.
- Cupcakes baked in wafer cones
- Root beer floats
- Homemade ice cream served in sugar cones (Invite guests to make the ice cream.)
- Taffy made at a taffy pull (See Theme-Inspired Activities.)

PARTY FAVORS AND PRIZES

- Pinwheel
- Bag of marbles
- Homemade taffy in a decorative bag
- Hard candy in a sugar cone (Wrap cone in cellophane and tie with ribbon.)
- Gift certificate to an ice-cream parlor

GIFT SUGGESTIONS

- Scrapbook with an ice-cream motif featuring photos of family members
- Black-and-white photo of the family dressed in late-1800s costumes, placed in an antique frame (See Theme-Inspired Activities.)
- Porch swing
- CD or cassette of barbershop music

Centenarian Celebrations

The one hundredth birthday is the pinnacle of milestone birthdays, and more and more people are celebrating it. The United States Census Bureau reports that the number of centenarians has nearly doubled in the last decade, and thanks to healthier lifestyles and breakthrough medical technologies, it expects that number to grow exponentially in the next century. But even though hundred-year-olds aren't the novelties they once were, someone of this age certainly deserves a special party, one that celebrates the rarity of his or her longevity.

Choose a celebration that fits the centenarian. Host a simple brunch at his or her home. Or invite him or her to a special family dinner. Maybe a family picnic or another larger affair is more appropriate. You know the honoree best. However you choose to celebrate, you can adapt any of the following theme parties to fit your situation and still host one of the most memorable occasions ever!

Before you begin planning your celebration, keep the following suggestions in mind:

Customize the Time and Duration of the Party

Keep the party time short and have the celebration when it's most convenient for the honoree. Some centenarians feel energetic in the morning, while others feel peppy after an afternoon nap. Because the honoree may tire easily, plan for the most important activities to occur early on. For example, have the honoree blow out birthday candles first. Have him or her open a few presents at the party and save the rest for a later date. Or ask a few guests to open gifts for the honoree.

Customize Party Etiquette

Consult with the honoree about the size of the guest list. If appropriate, make the celebration an open house in which guests arrive and leave at different times throughout the party. For example, invite neighbors to come from 11:00 A.M. to 1:00 P.M., church or synagogue members from noon to 2:00 P.M., and bridge club or senior center friends from 1:00 P.M. to 3:00 P.M. Provide a comfortable spot for the honoree to receive guests. Allow him or her to mingle at his or her own pace. Adjust music levels so conversations can be easily heard. Encourage the honoree to participate in activities at his or her own comfort level, even if that means just watching.

Customize the Refreshment and Menu Ideas

Serve refreshments when the honoree normally eats. When planning the menu, keep in mind that some guests may have special diets. If you don't know the dietary needs of guests, serve a variety of neutral foods (not too spicy, and so on) and label the menu items clearly. For the convenience of elderly guests, serve a sit-down meal. If you prefer to serve a buffet, however, recruit several helpers to assist or serve infirm or handicapped guests.

Arrange for a Special Escort

Don't let the party overshadow the honoree, who can get lost in all the activity. Assign a special escort or two to keep the honoree company, help him or her mingle, and provide assistance as necessary.

Royal Centenarian Celebration

Honor the remarkable gentleman or lady with a celebration fit for a king or queen.

INVITATIONS

Use formal invitations. On the inside engrave or write:

You're Invited
to a Royal Centenarian Celebration
in Honor of
[Name]'s
One Hundredth Birthday.
Please Join Us on [Date]
at [Time]
[Address]

Or consider these invitation designs:

- Fold cardstock in half. On the front, glue a recent photo of the honoree or one of him or her as a child. Write party details inside.
- Buy a birth date history printout for the honoree (available at party stores.) Roll it and the invitation together into a scroll and tie with ribbon. For added fun, incorporate a few details from the printout into the party details.
- Paint "100" and a crown on a small stone. Attach the invitation to it and add a note that reads "Celebrate [Name]'s Milestone 100th Birthday!"
- Have a photo of the honoree transferred onto a T-shirt and add the words "My Favorite Centenarian." Invite guests to wear the T-shirts to the party.

DÉCOR

- Adorn the honoree with a crown, robe, and scepter. Construct an arch over the honoree's "throne" at the head table. Decorate the arch and throne royally.
- Play CDs or cassettes of the honoree's favorite music in the background.
- Hang a banner of birthday wishes on the wall. Float a hundred colorful helium-filled balloons tied with ribbon.
- Tape "100" poster board cutouts to the walls and drape twisted streamers between the cutouts.
- Write seating assignments on party hats. Set them on a table near the entrance.
- Display photos of the honoree from each year of his or her life.
- Use paper tablecloths with a birthday motif. Or write "Happy 100th Birthday!" with metallic fabric paint onto organza and use as tablecloths. For family tables, make a family tree tablecloth for each branch of the family: Using fabric paint or cloth appliqués, design a tree in the center of a tablecloth. Write the honoree's name on the top branch. Have family members sign their names on the branches using a fabric pen. For a special touch, embroider the names after the party and give to the honoree.
- Slip a "My Favorite Centenarian" T-shirt (photo facing out) over each chair back. (See Invitations.)
- Write "100" on small inflated balloons. Glue the balloons into wafer cones and set one at each place setting.
- Place English party crackers (wrapped tubes containing small favors) at each place setting.
- Assign someone to attend to the king or queen throughout the party. Don't forget to bow or curtsy to royalty!

THEME-INSPIRED ACTIVITIES

- Have a birthday-card drawing: Number several birthday cards and place one under each plate. Number slips of paper to match the numbered cards and put them in a bowl. Draw a slip and award a prize to the guest with that numbered card. Or write "100! You're a Winner!" on a few of the birthday cards and award prizes to their owners.
- Make a birthday time capsule: Fill a container with heirlooms, novelties of the time, personal mementos, and a note from the honoree. Store the capsule until the birthday of the family's next centenarian.
- Make a centenarian celebration video: Videotape the party fun and best wishes from guests. Record the honoree telling the secret to longevity, his or her favorite moments in life, and what he or she wishes for the future. Watch the video at the end of the party.
- Make a family tree: Hang a large cloth or paper tree on a wall. Write the honoree's name on the top branch. Glue small Velcro strips onto the branches. Give each guest a leaf-shaped name tag with a small Velcro strip glued onto the back. Provide decorating supplies, such as glitter, stickers, and markers, and invite guests to decorate their name tags. Have guests stick their name tags onto the tree. Even if guests aren't related to the honoree, they're still part of his or her family of loved ones and should be included. Or plant a tree in the centenarian's honor. Photograph him or her digging the ceremonial first shovel full of dirt with a ribbon-tied shovel. Have guests use ribbon to hang their name tags from the branches.
- Have a royal centenarian ceremony: Have guests read the honoree's favorite poems or read poems about him or her. Present the honoree with a commemorative plaque. Invite his or her spiritual advisor to offer a blessing or say a special prayer.

MENU IDEAS

- Champagne Soup (See recipe below.)

  4 papayas
  ⅓ cup fresh lime juice
  ¼ cup honey
  1¼ cup orange juice
  1 bottle (750 ml) champagne

Purée papaya pulp. In large bowl, combine papaya with lime juice, honey, and orange juice. Chill overnight. Pour champagne into mixture just before serving. Add splash of champagne to each bowl at serving.

- Tossed green salad
- Dish of the Century (honoree's favorite dish)
- Homemade noodle stroganoff
- Mixed vegetables
- Crescent rolls with star-shaped pats of butter

DESSERT IDEAS

- Cake decorated with sparklers (See Supplier Resource Directory.)
- Tiered cake decorated with edible fourteen-carat gold foil accents
- Ice cream with candy confetti
- Minty Pears and Ice Cream: Set pear halves in dessert goblets. Scoop vanilla ice cream onto pears. Pour 1 tablespoon crème de menthe over each scoop and add whipped cream.

PARTY FAVORS AND PRIZES

- Photo button of the honoree
- Coffee mug with a photo of the honoree transferred onto it
- 100th Milestone: Paint "100" onto a small stone.

GIFT SUGGESTIONS

- Embroidered or photo family tree or family reunion photo
- Ink drawing of the honoree's childhood home, first home, or favorite retreat
- One hundred flower bulbs or perennials planted in the honoree's garden
- Public acknowledgment, such as the following:
    - Have the honoree's birthday acknowledged in a local newspaper. Most newspapers include a photo of the centenarian with the announcement. Find out early what the procedure is for submitting an announcement to ensure it's printed in time. Also, share the news with the honoree's clubs, associations, place of worship, and other organizations that may want to acknowledge him or

her. A local television station may also want to feature a story about the honoree.

- Contact the honoree's congressperson or senator well in advance and request that an American flag be flown on his or her hundredth birthday on a state or national building. The honoree may receive a flag and a certificate noting the date it was flown and in whose honor.
- Contact the president of the United States or the honoree's state governor well in advance and request a congratulatory note. (See Supplier Resource Directory.)
- Pool contributions from the guests and donate the money to charity in honor of the centenarian. Or recruit guests to volunteer at a shelter in his or her honor.

Person of the Century

Someone turning one hundred is definitely front-page news! Stop the presses and plan a great party for the Person of the Century.

INVITATIONS

Use invitations with a newspaper motif. On the inside write:

Extra! Extra! Read All about It!
[Name] Declared
Person of the Century!
You're Invited to
a Hot-off-the-Press
100th Birthday Party
on [Date] at [Time]
[Address]

Or consider these invitation designs:

- Have the invitation printed on newsprint. Or find a front page from a local newspaper. On a sheet of paper, write or type "Person of the Century!" in big block letters. Trim the statement to fit over the headline. Write party details on another sheet of paper and center it over the text below the headline. Photocopy the invitation.
- Glue a photo of the honoree on a note card. Print "Person of the Century" below the photo and write party details inside.

Whichever invitation design you choose, include a note inviting each guest to wear fashions from a decade in the honoree's life.

DÉCOR

- Recruit volunteers to dress in newsboy costumes and welcome guests. Have them pass out seating assignments and/or party favors from canvas newspaper bags.
- Hang an enlarged photo of the honoree on the wall. Add the caption "Person of the Century."
- Make an arch of black and white balloons. Set it at the entrance.
- Tape newspaper headlines from the last century to the walls. Use copies of actual front pages or write them on small banners. Hang photos of the honoree taken throughout the years.
- Hang two clotheslines diagonally across the ceiling and hang newspapers over them.
- Display magazines and newspapers from the last century on a newsstand.
- Use black tablecloths and white napkins on some tables. Use white tablecloths and black napkins on others. Or spread newspapers over tables and cover them with clear plastic tablecloths. Use napkin rings made from laminated newspaper strips.
- Decorate each table to represent a different decade from the honoree's life. For example, use pink tablecloths, black napkins, and 33⅓-rpm-record place mats for a 1950s table. Use photos of the honoree taken during the 1950s as a centerpiece.
- Before the party, write a newsletter that features stories about the honoree's life. Roll copies of it into scrolls, tie with ribbon, and set one at each place setting.

THEME-INSPIRED ACTIVITIES

- Ask two guests, a "reporter" and a "photojournalist," to canvass the party for scoops about the honoree. Have them videotape their interviews with guests. Show the video for the honoree during the party.
- Hold a centenarian trivia contest: Write interesting bits of information about the honoree's life, such as "Where did [Name] attend college?" as questions on slips of paper. Put the slips into a bowl. Divide the players into teams. Have a player draw a slip and read the question to his or her team. If the team can't answer the question within an allotted time, the other team tries to answer. Award a point for each correct answer and award prizes to the team with the most points.

- Give guests black markers and pieces of paper the size of a newspaper headline. Ask each guest to write headline birthday wishes. Have guests read their headlines aloud. Glue the headlines into a scrapbook for the honoree.
- Hire a deejay or band, clear a dance floor, and let guests dance to tunes recorded during the last century. Or rent a player piano for a sing-along.

MENU IDEAS

Serve these breakfast dishes, perfect complements to reading newspapers:

- Hotcakes and maple syrup
- Scrambled eggs
- Bacon and sausage
- Hash browns
- Toast and jam
- Coffee and orange juice

DESSERT IDEAS

- Cake with a photo of the honoree transferred onto it and the caption "Person of the Century"
- Cake decorated with a newsboy holding a newspaper and announcing, "Extra! Extra! [Name] Declared Person of the Century!"
- Ice-cream scoops

PARTY FAVORS AND PRIZES

- Hot-off-the-Press T-shirt: Bring in a vendor to silk-screen commemorative T-shirts.
- Small box of chocolates or candies wrapped in newspaper and tied with black ribbon
- Framed photo of the honoree captioned "Person of the Century"

GIFT SUGGESTIONS

Use newspaper to wrap any of these gifts:

- Commemorative "Person of the Year" plaque
- Newspaper subscription
- Newspaper or magazine from the day or month of honoree's birth

- CDs or cassettes of music from the last century
- Family newspaper: Have each branch of the family bring a letter highlighting what its members have been doing, what they plan to do, and so on. Have each also bring a note of best wishes for the honoree. Bind the letters and notes together, adding a "front page" featuring a photo of the honoree and an explanation of what's inside.

An Unconventional Garden Party

In her poem "Warning," Jenny Joseph expresses that growing old means earning the right to toss convention aside. Take inspiration from her words and throw an unconventional garden party for the uncommon centenarian.

INVITATIONS

Use purple-colored invitations. On the inside write in purple:

"When I am...old...I shall wear purple..."
—from "Warning" by Jenny Joseph

You're Invited to an
Unconventional Garden Party
in Honor of
[Name]'s
One Hundredth Birthday
on [Date] at [Time]
[Address]

Or consider these invitation designs:

- Write party details on a purple poster board cutout of a hat.
- Attach the invitation to a photo of the honoree wearing a purple outfit and red hat.
- Enclose a copy of Joseph's poem.
- Attach the invitation to a summer glove. Or write party details on a white poster board cutout of a glove.

Whichever invitation design you choose, include a note inviting guests to wear red or purple hats.

DÉCOR

Hold the party in a garden. Or create a garden indoors:

- Set potted trees and potted purple and red flowers around the room. Drape long purple ribbons or streamers over the branches.

- Make large flowers out of purple tissue paper and hang them from tree branches or attach them to fences or chair backs. Make smaller flowers to tie with purple ribbon around napkins.
- Use purple tablecloths. Hang red hats on novelty hat stands and use as centerpieces. Or place bouquets of red and purple flowers in the hats.
- Make a When I Am Old centerpiece: All over a hatbox, make a decoupage using copies of Joseph's poem. Set a bouquet of red roses in the box. Accent with pairs of summer gloves and satin sandals.
- Set bouquets of flowers picked from "other people's gardens" in empty brandy bottles. Set a sign that reads "These flowers came from [Guest's Name]'s garden. Thank you!" next to each bottle.
- Place a copy of Joseph's poem and a purple or red flower on each plate.
- Attach each place card to a summer glove or a satin sandal.

THEME-INSPIRED ACTIVITIES

- Read aloud Joseph's poem to set the mood.
- Make When I Am Old pledges: Give guests pencil and paper. Ask each to write a pledge like "When I am old I will walk barefoot on a white sandy beach" or "When I am old I am going to get a tattoo." Have guests read their pledges aloud. Have them vote for the pledges that are the Most Daring, Most Responsible, Most Fantastical, and so on. Award prizes to the winners.
- Play Musical Hats: Before the game, ask guests to give you the hats they wore to the party. Number small pieces of masking tape and stick them inside the hats. Number slips of paper to match the tape pieces and put them in a hat. Have players put on their hats and sit in a circle. When the music begins, players keep passing the hats to the players on the right. When the music stops, the players put on the hats they end up with. Draw a slip, read the number on it, and award a prize to the player with that number in the hat on his or her head.
- "Learn to Spit": Hold a watermelon-seed-spitting contest and award prizes to the players who spit seeds the farthest or onto targets marked on the floor.

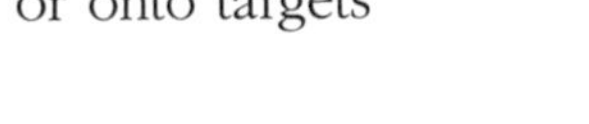

MENU IDEAS

- Brie garnished with purple grapes
- Eggplant bowls: Hollow out eggplants and fill with crab salad.
- Tossed salad garnished with purple onion slices
- Grape Jell-O squares topped with mayonnaise
- Blueberry muffins
- Grape juice
- Purple Fancy Punch: Mix 2 chilled bottles (each 750 ml) claret, 2 chilled 2-liter bottles ginger ale, and 2 trays of ice cubes in large punch bowl.

DESSERT IDEAS

- Purple cake or cupcakes with purple frosting topped with purple jellybeans or gumdrops (Add purple food coloring to white cake batter and white frosting.)
- Cheesecake topped with blueberry glaze
- Blueberry pie
- Flaming ice cream: Scoop vanilla ice cream into bowls. Pour 1 teaspoon brandy over each scoop and ignite before serving.
- Grape snow cones

PARTY FAVORS AND PRIZES

- Real or silk flower with a note card that reads "Pick the flowers in other people's gardens."
- Jar of grape jelly
- Purple scarf or hankie
- Photo of the honoree wearing a purple outfit and red hat

GIFT SUGGESTIONS

- Purple accessory, such as a handbag, tie, or scarf
- Bouquet of purple and red flowers
- Book of poetry by Jenny Joseph
- Piece of jewelry made with a purple gem

Shower of Birthday Wishes

Organize a card shower in which guests send the honoree birthday cards—perfect for centenarians who are homebound, ill, or feel that receiving lots of cards from loved ones is enough excitement. However, if the honoree would enjoy visiting with friends and family, a birthday card party complements this celebration perfectly.

INVITATIONS

Use invitations with an umbrella motif. On the inside write:

[Name]
Is Turning One Hundred!
Let's Celebrate
with a
Shower of Birthday Wishes.
Please Send [Him or Her] a Birthday Card
to
[Address]
to Arrive on or before [Birthday Date]

If you're also throwing a card party, write:

Then Join Us for a
Birthday Card Party
on [Date], [Time]
[Address]

Or consider these invitation designs:

- Invite guests by phone or by e-mail.
- Attach a birthday candle and a note that reads "Blow [Name] a 100th birthday wish!" to the invitation.
- Attach a drink umbrella to the invitation.

Whichever invitation design you choose, consider recruiting volunteers to help with the invitations. For example, invite friends and family to an invitation party to help make and address invitations. Provide food and music along with the invitation supplies. Or give each volunteer a list of phone numbers or e-mail addresses or an invitation kit containing invitations, inserts, postage, pen, and portion of the guest list. Have him or her contact the people on the list.

Or contact guests with a progressive invitation: Mail the invitation to the first person on the list. Include a note asking him or her to mail the invitation, the list, and a note explaining the procedure to the next person on the list. If the guest list is large, divide it among a few volunteers and have each mail the progressive invitation to the first person on his or her list.

DÉCOR

Keep the decorations simple:

- Use festive paper tableware and toss a few balloons around the room.
- Display the birthday cards in a decorated basket.
- Use the birthday cake as a centerpiece.
- Set favors at place settings. (See Party Favors and Prizes.) Tie ribbon around or a balloon to each favor.

THEME-INSPIRED ACTIVITIES

- Have a card-opening ceremony: Ask the centenarian not to open the birthday cards before the party and to bring them to the celebration. Pass out letter openers to the guests and have them open and read the cards aloud one at a time. Or if the honoree doesn't want to wait to open the cards, have him or her bring them to the party and let the guests read them aloud.
- Make a card scrapbook: Have guests glue the cards into a scrapbook. Provide scrapbook materials for guests to decorate the pages on which their cards appear.
- Let guests sign one big card: Make a big birthday card by folding a 2-by-3-foot sheet of newsprint. Decorate it and ask each guest to write best wishes on it.

MENU IDEAS

- Sandwiches cut into quarters, each decorated with a drink umbrella
- Relish tray
- Fruit-salad-on-a-stick: Stick fruit pieces onto skewers.
- Chips or pretzels
- Lemonade, iced tea, and water

DESSERT IDEAS

- Cake decorated to look like an umbrella or a greeting card
- Oatmeal cookies
- Ice-cream cookie sandwiches
- Umbrella ice-cream treats: Scoop ice cream into paper cups. Stick a candy cane into the center of each to look like an umbrella handle.

PARTY FAVORS AND PRIZES

- Pen tied with ribbon
- Letter opener
- Rubber ducky
- Bottle of shower gel

GIFT SUGGESTIONS

- Stationery set
- Umbrella
- Centenarian Cookbook: Gather the honoree's favorite recipes. Print the book by hand or by using a computer. Or use a printing service (see Supplier Resource Directory).
- Shower gift basket including shower gel, shampoo, shower cap, back scrubber, shower radio, plush towel and bathrobe, and so on

Supplier Resource Directory

Find any of the party supplies listed in *Memorable Milestone Birthdays* at your local party or craft supply stores, stationery or gift stores, import stores, bakeries or cake supply stores, floral shops, rental stores, decorating and prop companies, department or discount stores, specialty stores, and other retail establishments. Many of these businesses also offer party planning assistance.

Novelty items are also sold in specialty catalogs and on numerous sites on the World Wide Web. Find inexpensive party supplies at local thrift shops, flea markets, or garage sales. Antique shops and Grandma's attic may also contain treasures. And don't forget to use your imagination to make your own party supplies.

If you're unable to find a particular product, contact its manufacturer for a list of retailers near you. Some businesses may require quantity or wholesale purchases. If this is the case, ask a local retailer, party planner, or service vendor to order the product for you.

SPECTACULAR PARTY TOUCHES

The Butterfly Celebration

Address: Insect Lore, Post Office Box 1535, Shafter, California 93263
Phone: 800-548-3284
Fax: 661-746-0334
Web site: www.butterflycelebration.com

Release live butterflies for a unique and environmentally friendly presentation. You'll receive butterfly chrysalides, hatching boxes, bows to secure the boxes, a butterfly incubation tray, and complete instructions.

Maskparade: Custom Life-Size Face Masks on a Stick

Address: Patty Sachs' Celebration Creations, 14335 Ella Boulevard #1102, Houston, Texas 77014
Phone and Fax: 815-846-7460
Web site: www.pattysachs.com

Surprise the honoree with his or her own face! Give guests hand-held masks made from full-size photocopies of the honoree's face. The masks are mounted on poster board and trimmed with eyeglasses, jewelry, hair, neckties, and so on. They also make delightful programs, menus, or table decorations.

SongSendsations: Custom Songs for Special Occasions

Address: Patty Sachs' Celebration Creations, 14335 Ella Boulevard #1102, Houston, Texas 77014

Phone and Fax: 815-846-7460

Web site: www.listen.at/songsendsations

Have a personalized song parody written for the honoree. You'll receive a professionally recorded cassette along with a framed commemorative song sheet.

Sparktacular

Address: 5460 State Road 84, Bay #12, Fort Lauderdale, Florida 33314

Phone: 877-792-1101, 954-792-1101

Fax: 954-792-1837

Web site: www.sparktacular.com

Glitzzz Super Sparklers will ignite at just the right moment for forty-five seconds of brilliant excitement. Contact this company for a vendor near you.

DECORATING WITH FLAIR

Chocolates à la Carte

Address: 13190 Telfair Avenue, Sylmar, California 91342-0357

Phone: 800-966-7440, 800-818-2462, 818-364-6777

Fax: 818-364-8303

Web site: www.chocolates-ala-carte.com

This company makes creative molded chocolates, such as chocolate Cinderella slippers.

Harley-Davidson, Inc.

Address: H-D Customer Service, 3700 West Juneau Avenue, Milwaukee, Wisconsin 53208

Phone: 800-LUV-2-RIDE, 414-343-4056

Web site: www.roadstore.harley-davidson.com

Request a catalog or visit the on-line store for Harley-Davidson accessories, gifts, and collectibles. Or search on-line for a retailer near you.

Kentucky Derby Museum
Address: 704 Central Avenue, Louisville, Kentucky 40208
Phone: 800-593-3729
Web site: www.derbymuseum.org

Request a catalog or visit an on-line store filled with Kentucky Derby gifts and collectibles.

Victorian Trading Company
Address: 1819 Baltimore Avenue, Kansas City, Missouri 64108-0193
Phone: 800-700-2035
Web site: www.victoriantradingco.com

This catalog offers charming Victorian gifts and tea party accessories.

INVITATIONS AND PARTY FAVORS

The Adventure Group, Inc.
Address: 4720 Yender Avenue, Lisle, Illinois 60532
Phone: 630-960-5400

This company sells numerous unique containers perfect for invitations and party keepsakes. Call the number above for a list of retailers near you.

Bridalink
Phone: 800-725-6763
Web site: www.bridalink.com

Order a pack of six silver-plated cake charms to use in a Victorian birthday cake activity.

Cookbook Publishers, Inc.
Address: Post Office Box 15920, Lenexa, Kansas 66285-5920
Phone: 800-227-7282, 913-492-5900
Fax: 913-492-5947
Web site: www.cookbookpublishers.com

This company will print your family recipes in a personalized cookbook. Contact them for a free cookbook kit and price list.

Old Kentucky Candies
Address: 450 Southland Drive, Lexington, Kentucky 40503
Phone: 800-786-0579, 859-278-4444
Web site: www.oldkycandy.com

This company is best known for its Bourbon Chocolates, Derby Mints, Chocolate Thoroughbreds and Old Fashion Pulled Creams. The candies make great Derby Day party favors and treats.

MISCELLANEOUS RESOURCES

The Harry Fox Agency, Inc.
Address: NMPA/HFA, 711 Third Avenue, New York, New York 10017
Phone: 212-370-5330
Fax: 212-953-2384
Web site: www.nmpa.org

Contact this agency for information on licensing copyrighted musical compositions.

White House Greetings
Address: The President, Greetings Office, Room 39, White House, Washington, D.C. 20500
Fax: 202-395-1232

Have the president of the United States send a birthday greeting to a centenarian. In your request include the honoree's full name (including title), address, and birth date. The Greetings Office must receive your request at least six weeks prior to the occasion. Contact your state capitol for its procedure for governor greetings.

OTHER PARTY PLANNING PUBLICATIONS

The "Party" Chest Newsletter
Party Creations Book of Theme Event Design
Address: Clear Creek Publishing, Post Office Box 102324, Denver, Colorado 80250
Phone: 303-671-8253
E-mail: raksparkle@aol.com

This newsletter is packed with the latest industry news, party planning ideas, and supplier and service resources. A new theme design and catalog are included with each issue. Request a free sample copy.

This book contains sixty-seven complete, preplanned theme designs for unique and traditional events plus hundreds of innovative ideas for creating your own. Readers will find planning tips and forms, unique invitations, enchanting table decór, party game mixers, fun and festive activities, and easy yet elegant recipes.

Appendix

Cube Template

Enlarge as needed.

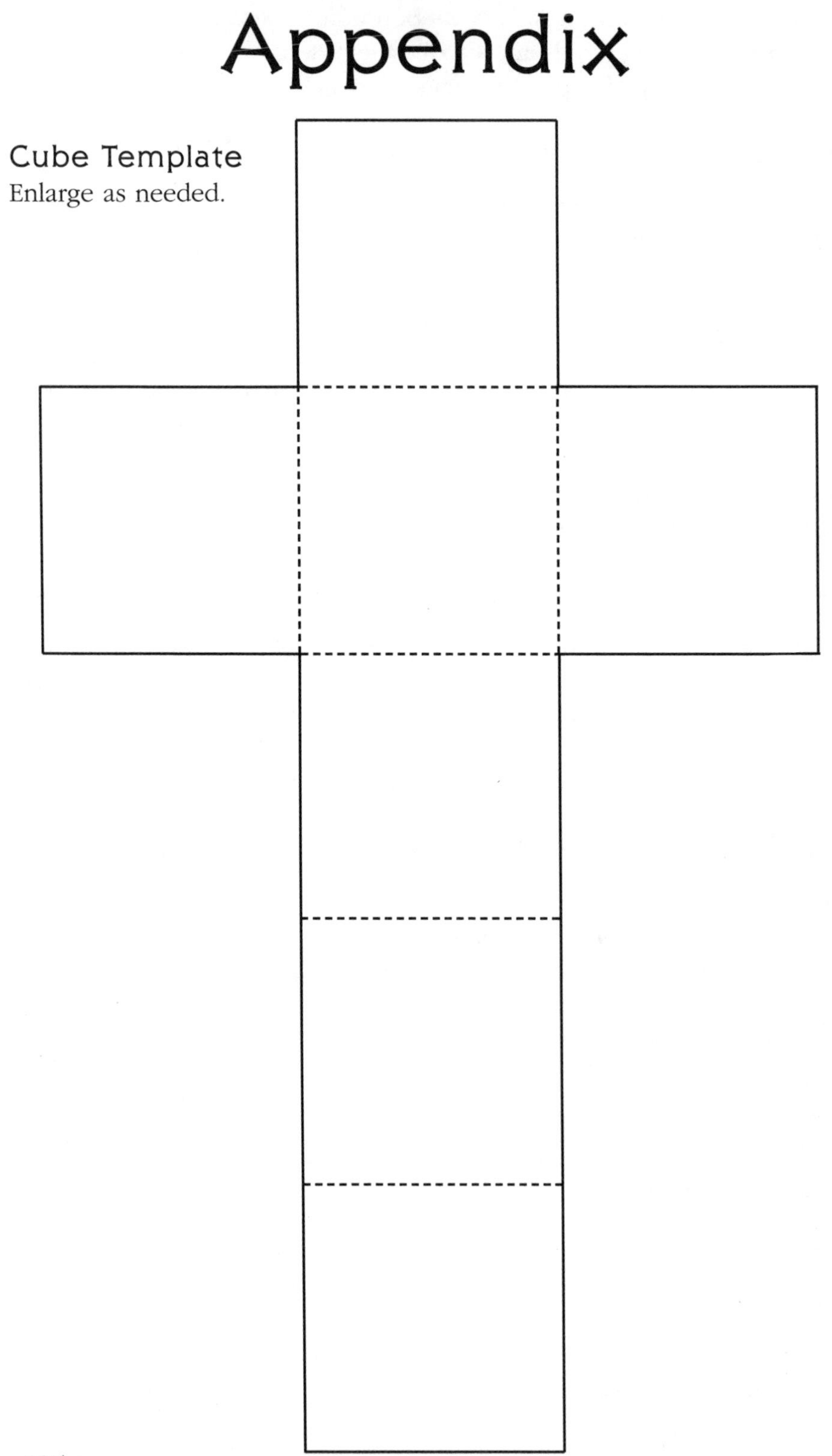

Index

Look for Meadowbrook Press books where you buy books. You may also order books by using the form printed below.

Order Form

Qty.	Title	Author	Order #	Unit Cost (U.S. $)	Total
	Age Happens	Lansky, B.	4025	$7.00	
	Are You Over the Hill?	Dodds, B.	4265	$7.00	
	52 Romantic Evenings	Oertel, L.	1213	$10.00	
	Baby Birthday Parties	Warner, P.	6050	$8.00	
	Best Party Book	Warner, P.	6089	$9.00	
	Best Baby Shower Book	Cooke, C.	1239	$7.95	
	Best Baby Shower Party Games #1	Cooke, C.	6063	$3.95	
	Best Bachelorette Party Book	Long, B.	6071	$7.95	
	Best Bachelorette Party Games	Cooke, C.	6073	$3.95	
	Best Bridal Shower Party Games #1	Cooke, C.	6060	$3.95	
	Best Wedding Shower Book	Cooke, C.	6059	$7.95	
	Complete Wedding Planner	Gilbert, E.	6005	$15.00	
	Dinner Party Cookbook	Brown, K.	6035	$9.00	
	Fun Family Traditions	MacGregor, C.	2446	$9.00	
	Games People Play	Warner, P.	6093	$8.00	
	Happy Anniversary!	Kring, R.	6041	$9.00	
	How to Survive Your 40th Birthday	Dodds, B.	4260	$7.00	
	Joy of Grandparenting	Sherins/Holleman	3502	$7.00	
	Joy of Marriage	Dodds, M. & B.	3504	$7.00	
	Joy of Parenthood	Blaustone, J.	3500	$7.00	
	Pick a Party	Sachs, P.	6085	$9.00	
	Pick-a-Party Cookbook	Sachs, P.	6086	$11.00	
	Something Old, Something New	Long, B.	6011	$9.95	
	Storybook Weddings	Kring, R.	6010	$8.00	
	What's So Funny about Getting Old?	Noland/Fischer	4205	$7.00	
	What You Don't Know/Turning 50	Witte, P.D.	4217	$6.00	
				Subtotal	
				Shipping and Handling (see below)	
				MN residents add 6.5% sales tax	
				Total	

YES! Please send me the books indicated above. Add $2.00 shipping and handling for the first book with a retail price up to $9.99 or $3.00 for the first book with a retail price over $9.99. Add $1.00 shipping and handling for each additional book. All orders must be prepaid. Most orders are shipped within two days by U.S. Mail (7–9 delivery days). Rush shipping is available for an extra charge. Overseas postage will be billed. **Quantity discounts available upon request.**

Send book(s) to:

Name ______________________ Address ______________________

City ______________ State ___ Zip _______ Telephone (____)______________

Payment via:

❏ Check or money order payable to Meadowbrook Press

❏ Visa (for orders over $10.00 only) ❏ MasterCard (for orders over $10.00 only)

Account # ______________ Signature ______________ Exp. Date ______________

You can also phone or fax us with a credit card order.

A *FREE* Meadowbrook Press catalog is available upon request.

Mail to: Meadowbrook Press
5451 Smetana Drive, Minnetonka, MN 55343

Phone 952-930-1100 Toll-Free 800-338-2232 Fax 952-930-1940

For more information (and fun) visit our website:
www.meadowbrookpress.com